A LIGHT SHINES THROUGH US

A Nun, a Businessman, and the Power of Connection

JOE SWEENEY

A LIGHT SHINES THROUGH US: A NUN, A BUSINESSMAN, AND THE POWER OF CONNECTION

Cover photo: ID 12575862 © Erica Schroeder | Dreamstime.com

1405 SW 6th Avenue • Ocala, Florida 34471 • Phone 352-622-1825 • Fax 352-622-1875
Website: www.atlantic-pub.com • Email: sales@atlantic-pub.com
SAN Number: 268-1250

Library of Congress Cataloging-in-Publication Data

Names: Sweeney, Joe, 1958- author.
Title: A light shines through us : a nun, a businessman, and the power of connection / Joe Sweeney.
Description: Ocala, Florida : Atlantic Publishing Group, Inc., 2020. | Summary: "Looking back on his friendship with Sister Camille, Joe Sweeney imparts his advice on finding faith through connections"—Provided by publisher.
Identifiers: LCCN 2020003230 (print) | LCCN 2020003231 (ebook) | ISBN 9781620237489 (paperback) | ISBN 9781620237496 (ebook)
Subjects: LCSH: Kliebhan, Camille, Sister. | Franciscan sisters—United States—Biography. | Sweeney, Joe, 1958- | Businessmen—United States—Biography. | Christian life—Catholic authors.
Classification: LCC BX4705.K5735 S84 2020 (print) | LCC BX4705.K5735 (ebook) | DDC 271/.97302 [B]—dc23
LC record available at https://lccn.loc.gov/2020003230
LC ebook record available at https://lccn.loc.gov/2020003231

Printed in the United States

PROJECT MANAGER: Meaghan Summers
INTERIOR LAYOUT AND JACKET DESIGN: Nicole Sturk

According to Celtic spiritual tradition, the soul shines all around the body like a luminous cloud. When you are very open, appreciative, and trusting with another person, your two souls flow together. This deeply felt bond with another person means you have found your *anam cara*, or "soul friend." Your *anam cara* always beholds your light and beauty and accepts you for who you truly are. When you are blessed with an *anam cara*, the Irish believe, you have arrived at that most sacred place—home.

~John O'Donohue

If you are looking for an uplifting story filled with deep wisdom about the meaning and purpose of life, this book delivers it.

—Jack Canfield, Coauthor of the
#1 New York Times bestselling
Chicken Soup for the Soul series

We experience a more meaningful connection with God when we deepen our relationships with others whose beliefs may be different from ours. *A Light Shines Through Us* is about the positive power of an unlikely friendship between two people seeking to follow God's perfect example of unconditional love. This book will open minds and soften hearts.

—Ken Blanchard, Coauthor of
The New One Minute Manager®
and Leading at a Higher Level

Even in my darkest hours in a Nazi concentration camp, Light shone in unexpected places to sustain and strengthen me as I clung to life. *A Light Shines Through Us* emanates the beauty and power of a connection between two people exemplifying my life's motto, "Every day is a bonus!"

—Joe Demler, WWII Veteran and
concentration camp survivor

As a Navy SEAL, we are taught to get comfortable being uncomfortable. The same goes for life, sometimes to get into the light, we have to walk through the darkness. *A Light Shines Through Us* will help you illuminate your path.

— Brian Groce, Former Navy SEAL
& Microsoft Executive

Jesus, the light of the world, urged us as well to be lights. As my friend Joe Sweeney colorfully shows in this fine book, Sister Camille sure was!

—Cardinal Timothy Dolan,
Archbishop of New York

A Light Shines Through Us is a loving, real-life story about a nun and a businessman who dive deeply into their shared faith. Together they contemplate a wealth of spiritual wisdom to transform their lives in ways that can inspire greater love and connection in your life too.

—Father Richard Rohr OFM

I have always believed that divine healing light is within each of us at this very moment. Joe Sweeney takes readers on a journey to connect with their inner light and be transformed

—Rob Wergin, Energy Healer

A Light Shines Through Us reminds me of my favorite song, "This little light of mine, I'm gonna let is shine…" Joe and Sr. Camille inspire all of us to exude the love and wisdom of God to all we come in contact with.

—Father Anthony Zimmer,
Pastor St. Anthony on the Lake
Pewaukee, WI

The founders of Unity church, Charles and Myrtle Fillmore, believed that "it is necessary to give freely if we are to receive freely. The law of receiving includes giving. The knowledge that substance is omnipresent and that people cannot, therefore, impoverish themselves by giving (but rather will increase their supply) will enable us to give freely and cheerfully." I love the universal lesson from Sr. Camille: For it is in giving that we receive.

—Reverend Mary Gabrielson, Pastor Unity Church

There was once a nun and a businessman—sounds like a beginning to a joke. Instead, Joe Sweeney's latest work gives us a story of unconditional love, light, and transformation as we are reminded how supported we are by a Universal

Presence and our ability to choose daily to activate our unique potential. Divine! Powerful! Magnificent!

—Karen Mills-Alston, Best-Selling Author of
10 Principles for a Life Worth Living

In my book, *Spiritual Liberation: Fulfilling Your Soul's Potential*, I say, "We have been given this precious human incarnation in which each and every one of us is a candidate for enlightenment." *A Light Shines Through Us* is an enlightening work for all readers looking for insight and awareness.

—Michael Bernard Beckwith, Founder
and Pastor of Agape Church

TABLE OF CONTENTS

APPENDIX

INTRODUCTION

Have you ever noticed someone by their glow? It is as if you could almost see a light shining through them. They have a natural inner beauty, a magnetism, a radiant energy that lights up a room when they enter.

You've met a person like that — someone who makes you feel good in their presence. When they speak, people listen. They draw people and opportunities to them constantly. They almost seem to vibrate at another frequency, as if a divine light is shining through them.

That light? It's within you too. At times, it may seem to diminish; while at others, it can illuminate entire rooms, conversations, and others' lives.

This is the light I saw thirty-two years ago when I first met Sister Camille Kliebhan.

This book explains how an unexpected connection can transform your life. I was blessed to have someone like Sister Camille that I was fortunate enough to connect with and who transformed my life.

The opportunity for meaningful connection is open to all of us. You just never know when you're going to run into someone at the grocery store, at the gym, at a coffee shop, in any of your daily activities, even at your work, who can change you forever.

If we are open to this connection, powerful transformation is possible.

Knowing and loving Sister Camille reminds me of a quote about light from Albert Schweitzer.

> "At times our light goes out and is rekindled by a spark from another person. Each of us has cause to think with deep gratitude of those who have lighted the flame within us."

May this book open you to the possibilities of a divine connection with another that could transform you forever.

WHERE THEY TAKE YOU TO DIE

The call was not entirely unexpected. She was ninety-five, for God's sake. And I mean both reverently.

True, Sister Camille Kliebhan was old, but not really. Wrinkles. Grey curls escaping the nun's veil she always wore. A fractured hip in 2015 slowed her down some, but not by much. And that smile. Yes, technically she was an elderly, Catholic nun but fortunately, she never acted like one. I grew up in a devout Catholic household, number nine of nine sons (if there was ever a reason to spend tens of thousands of dollars in therapy try being the ninth son). Most of the nuns I knew were stern disciplinarians, who seemed heaven-bent on catching young hooligans before they grew up into full-blown mischief-makers. Most Catholics of my generation have felt the sting of a ruler wielded by an unforgiving nun. Sister Camille wasn't like that. She looked for the best in every person she met and usually found it. It's funny. When I first met her, she was old enough to retire from her position as president of Cardinal Stritch University. She was, certainly, a lot older than me. But I've never thought of her as old.

On the other hand, everything that Sister Camille did, she did for God's sake. Nuns do not marry, so that they can devote themselves entirely to God, and Sister Camille lived out that vow with the enthusiasm and joy that she found in serving others. She viewed her sixty-plus years in higher education as a mission or calling from God, believing that every interaction with students, faculty, colleagues, alumni, donors—anyone—was an opportunity to demonstrate God's love. At a fundraiser, just prior to her death when the pressure was on to get a new home built for the sisters that were so close to her she said, "Dearie, people say a lot, so I like to watch what they do and look for the good or God in their actions. God in others is where the magic lies, Joe." She epitomized the well-known words attributed to St. Francis of Assisi: "Preach the gospel at all times. When necessary, use words." You might have spent a couple of hours with her and never heard her mention God or the tenets of her Catholic faith, but you always went away convinced that through her you connected with a power or force bigger than yourself, and that power was good, wonderful, and inviting. Yes, she was a godly woman—a modern day saint if there ever was one—, but she wasn't stuffy or out of touch. For example, I think it was Sister Camille who taught me why the nuns at her convent were so peaceful: they lived out the Gospel according to the example of St. Francis, they prayed regularly, and most importantly they had no husbands. She laughed mercifully, a deep belly laugh, whenever she could poke fun at the stress husbands added to women's lives.

According to the call I received earlier, my dear Sister Camille was nearing the end of her journey, ready to transition into, well . . . we'll get to that later. Of course, my heart was heavy as I motored down Illinois Avenue on the south side of Milwaukee, our shared hometown. After she retired, she sold the little house on the North Shore she shared with her sister, Joanne, who died a few years earlier, donating the profits to the university she served and a children's center she and her sister founded. She then moved into Clare Hall on the campus of the Sisters of St. Francis of Assisi convent–in all places, St. Francis, Wisconsin.

I smiled to myself as I recalled my many visits with her there. Clare Hall served as a retirement home for about sixty Franciscan nuns—simple yet comfortable, and Sister Camille seemed pleased to be living there with the other sisters. I stopped by once a week unless I was traveling, and we developed a little ritual where I would join them for Mass in the gorgeous chapel, one of two at the convent, and then we would all head to the dining room for dinner. On one of my first visits, I went into the kitchen and asked the lady preparing dinner if it would be okay if I brought a little wine for the nuns.

"Oh of course," she smiled. "The sisters would really love that, and you know how much their laughter makes my heart sing while the wine makes their taste buds rejoice."

Getting ready for dinner...a ritual we would practice many times.

Truer words were never spoken. From then on, I would pick up a case of wine and before Mass I would go into the kitchen and get the wine glasses, set them up on the tables, and pour the wine into the glasses, so that it would be waiting for them after Mass. Then about halfway through our meal, Sister Camille would give me that look that said, "I think it's time," and I would grab two bottles, one white and one red, and go from table to table and ask, "Would you like a little more wine, sister?" They would always respond, "Just a wee bit," and then I'd fill the glass to the brim, which never seemed to bother them. It was a pattern I would repeat nearly every week for several years. In fact, if I had to miss a week because of business travel, at least one of the nuns would call to make sure I'd be back the following week. I guess you could say I was their enabler.

At one of my first visits to the convent, I asked Sister Camille how she liked her new home. "It's really quite nice," she explained, then narrowed her eyes and with a mischievous grin and leaned closer to my face, "Just don't let them put me in the motherhouse," she implored. "That's where they take the really old people, and I'm not quite ready to die yet."

I was on my way to the motherhouse.

The heavy leaden clouds rolling in from Lake Michigan on that November afternoon should have mirrored my spirits, but that wasn't the case. The closer I got to the convent, the more excited I got. I know that sounds odd, maybe even a little insensitive. But almost from the first time I met her some thirty years ago, that's the effect she had on me. I couldn't get enough of this diminutive woman who had accomplished so much yet lived so simply and exuded pure joy. I used to stop by the campus of Cardinal Stritch University on my way home from work and wander around for a while, especially when I was feeling down, hoping to run into her for just a few moments to bask in the love and light that seemed to emanate from her. Sometimes I felt like I was Luke Skywalker and Sister Camille was Obi-Won Kenobi, a great Jedi knight master and spiritual teacher who was guiding my life's journey. I promise I wasn't stalking her—cross my heart—it was more like Freddy Eynsford-Hill in the popular musical "My Fair Lady" who sang,

People stop and stare, they don't bother me
For there's nowhere else on earth that I would rather be
Let the time go by, I won't care if I
Can be here on the street where you live.

As I headed toward the convent, I knew she was approaching the end of her earthly journey, but that didn't change anything—I still couldn't wait to see her again. It wasn't, "Poor Sister Camille is dying, and this is going to be so hard for me." But rather, "I get to see my soulmate." Of course, I knew that this could be the last time I saw her in this world, and that reality carried with it a certain sadness. And yet, we had talked about death and dying so much that neither of us feared it; neither of us thought of it as the final chapter. I took great comfort in knowing that when she transitioned, we would continue our conversations.

I found my regular parking spot near Clare Hall and walked the short distance to the motherhouse, an ancient and decaying building that should have depressed me. This remarkable woman, who had wined and dined with celebrities, could have easily afforded a more elegant life in a nice retirement community in Florida, yet she chose to remain with her order—the Catholic Order of St. Francis of Assisi—until she took her last breath. I thought of all she had accomplished in her life: earned a Ph.D. from The Catholic University of America in Washington, D.C. and served Cardinal Stritch University for sixty years as a faculty member, head of her department, dean of students, president, and chancellor. She was the first woman to chair the Sacred Heart School of Theology (in a male-dominated Catholic church) and to serve as president of both the Wisconsin Foundation of Independent Colleges and the Rotary Club of Milwaukee. Whether it was a CEO capable of donating millions to her beloved school or a maintenance worker sweeping the lobby of the administrative offices, she treated each the same, with dignity and respect. She understood—and helped me understand—that our value as humans did not come from material possessions but from what we had deposited in the deepest recesses of our souls. Sister Camille not only carried a fortune in her heart, but also shared it generously with everyone she met.

As I entered the building and noticed the ever-present crucifix on the wall, my mind wandered to our many conversations about the church. Or rather, my increasing distance from organized religion. It all seems so ego-centric to me: "We're *Methodists,* not like those backward Baptists." Or "we're *Catholics,* the one true church." It seems to me that religious people are more concerned about being right than living out the teachings of their religion. I saw this a lot in my fellow Catholics. They would show up for Mass every Sunday and act all holy and pure and turn back into jerks the second they left the church. Instead of trying to correct my thinking or defending the church, she agreed with many of my criticisms of the church but gently reminded me that none of us is perfect. I remember the first time I confessed to her that my spirituality was being heavily influenced by the Buddha and the teachings of Lao Tzu, fully expecting a mile rebuke. "Oh dearie," she would say. "I don't have a problem with that. Wisdom can come from many sources, and whatever enhances the good of mankind has to be true. If it's making you a better person, it must be from God." Instead of correcting my wayward thinking, she encouraged me in my quest for truth, even examining the Tao Te Ching with me.

I found my way to her room and almost laughed at what I saw. Sister Camille was a lifelong, fanatical Green Bay Packers fan, and this was a Thursday night where they would be playing on national television. Sister Camille was not your ordinary rabid Packer fan (a redundancy, for sure). Her uncle, Adolph Kliebhan, was the first starting quarterback for the Pack. After a couple of bad games, however, he lost his starting job to another guy: Curly Lambeau. She always got her treasured Green Bay Packers blanket out for each game, and there she was, lying on her bed with the television on, clutching her blanket. They may have sent her here to die, but she wasn't cooperating very well. Most of the other nuns confined to the motherhouse were in various stages of dementia. Sister Camille may have been physically weak, but her mind was clear, and no one was going to stop her from enjoying what life she had left.

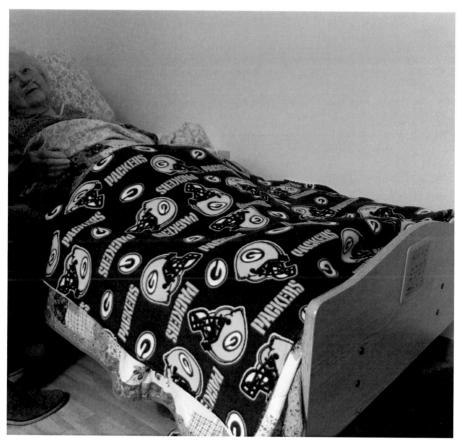

Sister enjoyed cuddling-up in her lucky Green Bay Packer blanket.

After greeting her, I knew what I had to do. I reached into a cabinet next to her bed and retrieved the bottle of gin I had placed there a few months back. Sister loved her gin martinis—two olives—,and whenever anyone rebuffed her for such an un-nun-like habit, she always responded, "I'm a human being, and I enjoy a gin martini. Sometimes two." And she did, so when she moved into the motherhouse where everything she ate or drank was closely monitored, I made sure she could still enjoy her martinis, even if her caregivers would have disapproved. I prepared her drink and set it on the nightstand, but she just let it sit there. "Not tonight—they've got me on medication." After adjusting her pillows and making sure she was comfortable, I sat next to her in a chair as we watched the Packers take the field in Seattle. How could anyone be sad on an occasion such as this?

Then things started to unravel.

First, the Packers fell behind quickly, and that never sits well with Sister. The only time I've ever seen her even close to being grumpy is whenever the Packers lose. She probably took those losses harder than the players, and things weren't looking good for the Pack. God, I hope they win tonight, if for no other reason than to make Sister happy.

Then, she complained of being cold. She had wrapped herself in that Packers blanket but was beginning to shiver. Her room was actually quite warm; I worried that maybe her body was shutting down, that maybe this is what happens just before someone dies. I know what happened next may sound weird, but I didn't hesitate. I got up from my chair, walked over to her bed, then gently climbed in beside her, wrapping my arms around her frail, shivering body, and held her close. A fifty-nine-year-old businessman. A ninety-five-year-old nun lying in bed in the motherhouse watching the Green Bay Packers on television. Not your everyday rendezvous, but to me it was maybe the most beautiful moment of all my treasured times with Sister.

For some reason, my mind went to a dreadfully hot and humid day in August when she was still living in her home. After her sister died, I tried to stop by a few times each week to see how she was doing or help out in any way she needed. I knocked on the screen door and heard her invite me in. It must have been a hundred degrees inside that house, but there was Sister scrubbing the kitchen floor. It was the only time I had seen her without her habit, until tonight. This courageous trailblazer—a true saint as far as I'm concerned—was growing weaker by the moment, and yet even as she lay nearly helpless in my arms, I could sense a quiet strength radiating from her soul. I remembered a conversation with her where she talked about learning how to die and now realized what a good student she was.

Soon, her shivering stopped, and her breathing slowed, and for a split-second I thought that she had lost consciousness. Should I ring for the nurse? Is she going to die right here in my arms? Then, as if aroused from a deep sleep, Sister made me laugh again.

"Is Aaron Rogers going to bring them back?"

My beloved friend wasn't ready to die just yet.

After midnight, it was time for me to go. Over the years we had developed a little ritual that we practiced whenever we parted company. We would hold hands, and then I would begin by saying, "The light of God." Then she would respond with, "Shines through us." I continued with, "The love of God," with Sister Camille adding, "Flows through us." Once again, I led with "We are rooted," followed by Sister affirming, "In divine love." Then together we would say, "For eternity. And so, it is."

I knelt next to Sister's bed, and we grabbed each other's hands. I looked down at her beautiful face, her eyes dancing with anticipation. I didn't know if I would ever see her again in this world, but it didn't matter. She had taught me to enjoy the now, to gather as much joy and pleasure as you can from even the simplest of things.

> The light of God
> Shines through us.
> The love of God
> Flows through us.
> We are rooted
> In divine love
> For eternity
> And so, it is.

I gently squeezed her hand, leaned over, and kissed her on the check, then slipped out of her room and into the hall wondering if I would ever return to the motherhouse, where they take only the really old people to die.

— 2 —

LOOKING FOR A GYM

I grew up in a wonderfully boisterous Irish-Catholic family in Madison, Wisconsin., the ninth boy out of ten kids. Try to imagine ten kids getting ready for school in the morning. Or sitting down at the dinner table. Or piling into the station wagon on Sunday mornings to try and get to Mass on time. Life with the Sweeneys might be described as organized chaos, but what a great blessing to be surrounded by so many siblings, to say nothing of two parents who loved us enough to not give us everything we asked for. It may not have been the ideal childhood, but it was close. I have no idea how my parents did it without the internet; I asked my nine siblings what our parents did with their time before the world-wide web, but I'm certain I already knew.

While I'm not all that old, I have to confess that when I was a kid, we didn't have those little screens that kids today bury their noses in practically twenty-four seven. And even if cell phones had been around when I was growing up, I doubt my parents would have been able to afford ten of them; even if they could, you can be damn sure they'd have pretty strict rules for when we could play with them. That didn't stop us from having fun. Just the opposite. When you don't have stuff to entertain you, what do you do? You find ways to entertain yourself, and for us, that meant sports. Even before we were old enough to join organized teams at school, there was hardly a day when we weren't out in the yard playing pick-up games of football or baseball or shooting baskets in the driveway. Being one of the youngest, I can't tell you how many times I ended up on my keister whenever we played football. Even though we always played "two-hand touch,"—instead of tackling the ball carrier, all you had to do was put two hands on him and the play was over—my brothers always seemed to "touch" me in such a manner that sent me flying. But I didn't care. I just loved all those afternoons and weekends competing against my siblings and the other kids in our neighborhood.

Although I loved all sports, my game was basketball. I couldn't get enough of it. If for some reason I couldn't get any of my brothers to join me in the driveway for a game of hoops, I'd scour the neighborhood, looking for a game to join. Or if I couldn't find a game, I'd grab a ball and work on my shot in our little driveway with the backboard and hoop attached to the garage. Rain or shine, blazing hot summer or frigid, snowy winter., it didn't matter. Once I got finished with my homework—okay, maybe a few times I ditched the homework—I'd head outside to shoot some hoops. I can't tell you how many times I'd work on my shot when the temperature hovered around zero and my hands would split from the cold, but I'd just keep shooting.

You might say I was a shootaholic, because of the time and effort I spent perfecting my shot. I loved shooting so much that I did my thesis on shooting. Even into adulthood I would spend an hour after work shooting in the driveway. It's how I relaxed.

I played high school basketball and had to really work hard at it because I was just a skinny white kid from a bad gene pool. I didn't earn a letter my junior year, and that made me so mad that I spent the entire off-season practicing, which paid off. I earned my letter, along with a few other extra honors. I also played a little in college, and while I was in graduate school, I joined a few industrial leagues. And while I enjoyed the competition, I discovered that the art of shooting a basketball became a form of relaxation for me. Some guys went to the bar for a couple of drinks to relax; I found a hoop and shot baskets for two hours. In high school, I hated geometry, but as I learned about backboard magic—banking the ball off the board at just the right angle, I fell in love with the subject. In fact, I loved shooting baskets so much that I found a way to turn that love into my undergraduate thesis titled *The Impact of Physical Relaxation and Mental Visualization on Athletic Performance*. And if that wasn't enough, I continue to work with a few college and high school basketball teams, helping the players perfect their free throw shooting.

After graduate school, I moved my little family to Waukesha, Wisconsin and began working for a small steel company that I would eventually buy from the owner who planned to retire in a few years. It was a great opportunity professionally, but this guy who grew up in a large family and was always surrounded by siblings and friends soon discovered how difficult it was for an Irish Catholic from "out of town" to make friends. It wasn't that the people there were particularly unfriendly. I just didn't realize how difficult it would be for an outsider to find a spot on the social landscape. I'd pretty much lived in one place all my life, and an out-of-towner moving into my hometown of Madison would probably face the same obstacles. I didn't know it at the time, but it takes time to put your roots down, and it wasn't long before I was feeling like a fish out of water. I needed the oxygen that my big family and familiar neighborhood gave me.

About that time, I became part owner of another company and moved twenty-five miles north to Fox Point, a suburb of Milwaukee. It was a great neighborhood of modest homes, except for one thing- no sidewalks. At least in Waukesha I could wave at people as they walked by on the sidewalk in front of our apartment. Here, once the neighbors got home from work and closed the garage door, you never saw them.

I felt like a part of me was dying.

Mostly just to maintain my sanity, but also because I still loved the game, I would head to a local park after work and shoot baskets. Great stress reliever, plus it momentarily took my mind off the reality that we were stranded on this desert island in the middle of a sea of neighbors. I'd throw up jump shots for about an hour or more, then trudge back home. I tried taking my two sons to the park to maybe get them to share my love of the sport, but I soon realized that even with their kid-sized basketballs, heaving them up to a ten-foot basket was just too much. If anything, it carried the risk of discouraging them from playing the game that I loved. I was about to give up on ever seeing my kids play basketball when a stroll through the warehouse of my company gave me an idea that you might say changed my life.

We manufactured a variety of equipment and accessories for the commercial photographic industry and for some reason—call it fate, karma, a God-thing, who knows—I walked past some tripods that we made for studio work. We offered them in four, six, eight, and ten-foot models, but that day all I could see were backboards attached to them so that any sized kid could enjoy the swish of a ball sliding through the basket. I got a hold of one of our engineers and shared my idea with him, and he went to work. A few weeks later he called me to the manufacturing floor to show me his design. I was so excited I could barely contain myself. There before me were four tripods, each with a shiny glass backboard, orange rim, and nylon net. I remembered the many public courts I'd played on where the net had disappeared either to the weather and overuse or from someone who wanted a new net for his backyard court. My kids were going to have the real deal.

I raced out back to get the company van, loaded up all four basketball stands formerly known as studio-camera tripods, product number MP4, MP6, MP8, and MP10, and drove the fifteen miles back to our home in Fox Point. I can only imagine what the neighbors thought as they watched me wrestle those big stands out of the van and set them up around the perimeter of our little driveway, but it didn't take long to find out what they *really* thought of this strange dude with the glass backboards. After a couple of days of taking my two boys out to shoot baskets on the four-foot basket, Ben, Ari, and Danny—sons of Rabbi Ron and Judy Shapiro—walked over and asked if they could shoot baskets with us. Are you kidding? Something of a frustrated basketball coach, I not only let them shoot around, but also began teaching them basic fundamentals of the game, always handing out an ice-cold Coke when were done.

News travels fast, even without sidewalks. Within a few days of setting up those baskets, a couple of dozen boys from the neighborhood were stopping by to give those nets a workout, and I loved every minute of it. I would organize various drills, then divide the older kids up and let them play half-court games. But here's the real payoff. Pretty soon, the kids' parents began stopping by just to hang out and talk. Add cold beverages and snacks to the mix and this guy who felt so isolated and alone was finally in his element.

It gets better.

As word spread, more than sixty kids began showing up. My little driveway was already too small for those first two dozen kids, but I couldn't turn away any kid who just wanted to shoot hoops at our place. I decided to create a basketball camp, but first I needed to find a bigger venue. I scouted around and considered one of the public parks, but what would happen if it rained? I needed a real gym, not just to avoid weather-related issues, but I wanted these guys to enjoy playing on a hardwood court, run up and down a full-sized court, and feel like real basketball players. I wanted them to experience a phenomenal basketball camp.– for free–, which meant I wouldn't be able to afford to pay very much to rent a real gym.

When I first moved to Fox Point, I noticed a sign not far from my house: Cardinal Stritch University. I didn't think much of it at the time, but in my quest for a real gym for my basketball camp, I couldn't get that school out of my mind. I learned that it was a Catholic university begun as a teaching institution for the Sisters of St. Francis of Assisi. I learned that it was named after Milwaukee's Archbishop Samuel Stritch, later to be appointed cardinal, and that it had grown from a small, insular college for women to a full-fledged university with an enrollment of 2,500 men and women. And I learned that the person responsible for most of that growth was its president, Sister Camille Kliebhan.

I wasn't born with the proverbial silver spoon, but my business was doing pretty well, and I'd managed to put some money away in a savings account. Probably not enough to rent a full-sized fieldhouse at a university, but I thought I might convince the president of a Catholic university to cut a sweetheart deal with a pretty normal Catholic who seldom missed Mass. With checkbook in hand, I drove the few minutes over to Cardinal Stritch University to meet the president who graciously gave me an appointment. I parked my car in the visitor's lot and walked into the spacious, airy reception area of one of the newest buildings on campus. The receptionist directed me to the president's office on the first floor. I practically ran down the hallway before catching my breath and walking through the door labeled "President." I introduced myself to a very polite lady sitting at a desk who smiled, "Oh, go right in. Sister's expecting you Mr. Sweeney."

The instant I entered Sister Camille's office, I knew she was different, but I can't say exactly how. For one thing, she didn't have that official or authoritative look. Nor did she have that stern look that I recalled from my twenty years of Catholic school, fourteen taught by nuns. Rather, she had the sweetest smile, along with the accompanying wrinkles that told me she did a lot more smiling than frowning. A good sign.

"Such a pleasure to meet you, Mr. Sweeney," she began as she got up from behind her desk to shake my hand.

"The pleasure is mine, Sister, but please call me Joe."

"Now what is it you'd like to talk about," she answered, and I noted that she didn't call me Joe.

She motioned for me to sit in a chair away from her desk and moved to sit in another one opposite me. Small matter, but over the years I've noticed that people who want to impress with their rank or title always remain behind their big corporate desks, where true leaders who care more about their customers or clients than status always move the conversation away from their desks. It sort of sends an important message: "You are important to me." Sister Kliebhan made it crystal clear that whatever I had to say, she was there to listen carefully and that time was not a factor.

I began by explaining how I had started a little basketball program in my driveway and how it had grown to the point that I needed to find a bigger place for them to play. I told her that I had a dream to offer state-of-the-art basketball camp, but that I didn't want money to stand in the way of any boy who wanted to attend ,so I wasn't planning on charging a fee for the camp. As I kept pitching the idea of a free basketball camp, she interrupted me.

"Would you like to see our gym?"

Would I? She got up and headed out through the outer office and down the stairway, turning left down a big hallway, winding around until we came to those sets of double doors you always see at a gymnasium. She held it open for me, and when I walked into that huge gym, I almost lost it. All I could see were fifty, sixty, maybe a hundred kids running up and down the immaculately varnished hardwood. Four games going on at once, the gym was that big.

"Do you think this would be big enough for your basketball camp?"

I could have hugged her, but I didn't think you're supposed to do that to a nun.

As we headed back upstairs to her office, my mind was spinning. With a facility like this, I would have no problem filling the gym. Then maybe instead of charging a fee, I would ask each kid to go door-to-door in their neighborhoods to appeal for pledges toward one of Milwaukee's biggest charities: Midwest Athletes Against Childhood Cancer. I began mentally doing the math to see how much I could afford and where I would get the rest once I learned how much it would cost to rent this beautiful facility.

We got back to her office and sat down once again, I continued where I had left off, which was sharing my vision for a world-class basketball camp. As I rattled on she smiled and nodded her head, and I began to think that maybe she would rent the gym to me. Finally, I swallowed hard and popped the question.

"Sister Camille, your gym would be the perfect setting for my basketball camp. Those kids won't believe their eyes when they first walk into it. And having showers and locker rooms will make them feel so important. You know, it's not just about basketball. I want to help develop positive values in them as they grow into young men. I'm definitely interested, but I do need to ask about your fee. How much would you charge to rent your gym for one week next summer?"

"Oh dearie," she smiled. "Just coordinate the dates with my assistant and you can use it. I wouldn't think of charging you."

A few minutes earlier, I wanted to hug her. Now I wanted to kiss her, but I was pretty sure you're not supposed to do that to nuns.

Feeling the checkbook holstered in my pocket to pay for the court time, I said, "Sister, I didn't come here to try and get something for nothing."

"Of course, you didn't, dearie. And you're not getting something for nothing. I know that running a camp like that takes a lot of work. And I know you'll give those boys an experience they'll never forget. If there's anything else you need, just let me know."

She was right. That camp required a lot of work, and I got a lot of help from some fantastic volunteers. Better yet, those kids really came through. I taught them to go door-to-door with this little appeal: "Ma'am, I'm going to basketball camp to help kids with cancer. I'm going to shoot two-hundred free throws while I'm there. How much will you sponsor me for each shot I make?" That first camp raised $10,000 and by the time we ended it a few years later, we had raised more than $100,000 for a great charity.

As I left her office and walked back to my car in the cool fall breeze coming off Lake Michigan, I was, of course, practically walking on air. Naturally, I was thrilled that I not only now had a gym for my basketball camp, but that I had gotten it free. But my exhilaration was not really about basketball, it was about that little nun with the beautiful smile who called me dearie. Even as I began making plans for the camp, recruiting volunteers, tackling the thousand-and-one details to make sure we were ready to go the next summer, I couldn't quit thinking about that diminutive nun who took time out of a busy schedule to meet with me. There was just something about her that I couldn't explain and couldn't escape.

In that brief exchange, it was clear that she wanted nothing from me; only wanted the best for others. That was so shockingly unfamiliar to me as a businessman. In all the deals and horse trading I did, you always made sure you got something in exchange for whatever you offered the other guy. I went into my meeting with Sister somewhat guarded, and she disarmed me with her honesty and grace. It made a huge impact on me, but something else happened, that is a little difficult to explain.

The whole time I was with Sister Camille, I felt incredible love emanating from her. It was truly a magnetic connection. When I looked at her, I actually saw a special light shining through her. A divine and human connection that I had never experienced or felt before.

It was as if that light was shining through both of us.

— 3 —

NOT LIKE MOST NUNS

I am what some people call a "cradle Catholic," meaning my parents took me to Mass very likely the first Sunday after I was born. I have twenty years of Catholic education under my belt: two years of Catholic kindergarten, eight years of Catholic grade school, four years of Catholic high school, four years of Catholic undergraduate school, and two years of Catholic graduate school. Like Sister Camille, who grew up in a devout Catholic family, I really didn't have any choice. Sister and I had strict, traditional, Catholic parents, and that dictated much of our lives when it came to school. I'm pretty sure my parents hoped all that Catholic teaching would turn me into a super Catholic maybe even a priest, something some Catholic parents privately wish would happen in their families. When it came to college and I had a little more freedom to choose, I still went to a Catholic school, not so much because I wanted to be a good Catholic but because St. Mary's was a small school where I knew I could play varsity basketball.

So much for my parents' dreams of me becoming a priest.

Ask any guy, who, like me, grew up in a Catholic home in the 1960s, what they remember most about school, and I'll guarantee they'll all give the same answer: the nuns. During my years from kindergarten through high school at Our Lady Queen of Peace elementary school, most of my teachers were nuns. And what I remember most about them was how strict they were, especially Sister Almadeo, my second grade teacher. I'll admit I was a bit of a smartass back then (and people who know me now say I haven't changed much), but we fought tooth and nail about everything. Our biggest battle exploded over original sin, a doctrine I still don't buy. We were all studying for First Communion, and Sister wanted to make sure we understood that all of us little eight-year-olds were sinners. Most of my classmates did the smart thing and just nodded their heads when she asked them if they were sinners, but I refused, which meant I was singled out for some one-on-one tutoring on the finer points of original sin.

"Joey, it's okay to admit that you're a sinner. We all are. I am. All the students here are sinners. Even Fr. Lovell is a sinner."

I just sat there stubbornly refusing to cave.

"But it's okay, Joey, because Jesus died for our sins."

"What?" I asked.

"That's right, Joey. Jesus died for your sins."

"For *my* sins?"

"Oh yes, Joey," she beamed, clearly pleased that she was making progress with me.

"Let me ask you something, Sister Almadeo."

"Why of course, Joey."

"How long ago did Jesus die for my sins?"

"Almost 2,000 years ago, Joey," she explained with great confidence that finally she was getting somewhere.

"But Sister," I protested. "I'm only eight years old. I wasn't even around then!"

If there ever was justification for getting the proverbial rap a nun's ruler, that was it, but thankfully, Sister Almadeo had mercy on my knuckles.

But they were all like that. Strict. Serious. In many ways, almost severe. Maybe even a bit masochistic, a drastic claim, but it's based on countless encounters with the various forms of punishment chosen by these nuns. And of course, we never complained to our parents, knowing full well that whatever punishment was doled out by our teachers would be doubled by Mom or Dad when we got home. Wisely, we took our medicine and kept our mouths shut.

By the time I got to high school, I was hungry to learn from others feeling like the nuns had instilled in me all the lessons needed to be a good person. As far as I was concerned, they were just part of the package in getting a really decent education, but you would never find me going out of my way to hang out with any of them. Until I got to high school. Remember, this was in the '60s and '70s after Vatican II, and a lot of priests and nuns got all caught up in peace and love and began holding guitar masses and dressing like hippies. Instead of the rigid nuns in habits of my earlier years, all of the sudden nuns not only seemed like real people, but also seemed pretty cool as well.

I'll never forget the time my brother had his backpack stolen at school, and we went to report it to Sister Serafica.

"Sister, someone stole my backpack, and it had all my homework in it, and I'm really pissed!" He was really angry, but I was ready to duck, certain that Sister would come out swinging at his potty mouth. Boy, were we surprised.

"Oh dear, Mark, "she began in a very sweet and non-threatening lilt. "There's no reason to be pee-issed."

We about died of shock, later laughing until we could barely keep from falling over.

Gradually, I began to rethink my viewpoint about nuns, a process that accelerated when I met Sister Alphonsine, my high school guidance counselor.

Instead of trying to catch me doing something wrong, like the grammar school nuns I encountered, Sister Alphonsine seemed to go out of her way to commend me for doing things right. She encouraged me to keep my grades up, not in a nagging way, but in a way that made me feel it was actually possible. But what I really loved about her is that she not only seemed to understand my addiction to basketball, she fed it. Countless times after hours and on weekends she would unlock the gym for me, so I could continue working on my shot. I repaid her, so to speak, by keeping her supplied with Jack Daniels, and that requires a little explaining.

Dear Sister Alphonsine suffered from throat and mouth cancer, which kept her in a perennial state of pain. I mean really bad pain. So, at first, I would drive her to the liquor store after school, so she could buy a fifth of Jack. Then when she discovered I had a fake ID, she would just hand me the money and I'd go buy it for her. Soon we developed a little routine. After school and basketball practice, I'd go home and eat and do my homework, then head back to the high school, sometimes as late as ten or eleven o'clock. I'd stop and buy her liquor, then she'd meet me at the gym and unlock it for me. She lived in a room high up in the towers of the high school, so when I finished shooting, she'd come down and close up the gym. Wow, have times changed.

With a much more generous view of nuns, I left high school and went off to St. Mary's for my undergraduate work and to Notre Dame for my master's degree, but for some reason, I never really had any more contact with nuns. At least not directly. Of course, I'd see them occasionally on both campuses, but never in the classroom. If you would have asked me at the time what I thought of nuns, I'd probably offer up mixed feelings: mostly a bunch of stern disciplinarians, with a few good ones who seem to have escaped the convent. And then I met Sister Camille.

Sister's educational journey was much the same as mine, attending Catholic schools, and she was encouraged by her parents to attend Cardinal Stritch College while working as an assistant for a law firm in Milwaukee. She also helped her father, Alfred Sebastian, a local banker learning the ropes of the financial industry; both of these jobs would later help Sister in her college leadership, business, and fundraising roles for years to come. While Sister had no predetermined or intended path to become a nun, she loved the Catholic community of sisters and was drawn to their Franciscan philosophy, humble in spirit, yet bold in action.

It's not that Sister Camille wasn't like any other nun I had ever met, she was unlike any other human being I had ever met. I know that sounds like an exaggeration, but it's true. For one thing, she was just really cool. By that I mean she was unflappable. No matter what situation she found herself in, she remained herself. She didn't try to act like a college president or a Catholic nun or anything else. She was so comfortable in who she was that it made being with her so easy. I walked into her office that first time thinking I had to put on some big show to impress her, and I walked out feeling as if I had just spent time with my best friend. Yet I barely knew her!

This may sound a little out there, but she also had an aura about her, and I'll try to explain it like this. Over my career, I've had the honor of meeting a number of what I would call really great people. Not just famous, but famous for all the right reasons. General Colin Powell comes to mind. The instant I met him I sensed something about him that set him apart from any other leader I've met. It was the same with Sister Camille, and I've come to identify that aura in terms of the soul. She was in her sixties when I first met her, and that quality of an older, mature, developed soul just exuded from her. She also possessed a quiet, soft strength about her.

Perhaps it was that developed soul that gave her such crystal-clear insights into what was right and prudent to do. One time, I was sharing with her some ideas that were bouncing around in my head and that I felt I wanted to write about in a book about networking.

"Tell me, dearie, what's the number one thing about networking?" she asked, as if I was the only person on her schedule that day and her entire reason for living was to help me sort through my confusion.

"Networking is the realization that it's not all about me," I began. "If you can help others get what they want, that's the way to connect with them. You actually help others to help yourself."

Her answer was a wise as it was concise.

"Well then, why don't you write your book based on the theme of the prayer of St. Francis: it is in giving that we receive."

Whoa! She nailed it. And even though I knew businessmen wouldn't buy a book about a saint, her insight helped me organize my thoughts around the dogma of that great prayer. Once I got that little detail out of the way, I whined to her about something else that was bothering me.

"Sister, to be perfectly honest, I have no idea how to write a book. I'm a bullet point kind of guy. I jot things down on scraps of paper and sketch out my ideas on the backs of napkins. I know I have something unique to offer, but how in the world am I going to write a book." Again, undaunted by my inexperience or insecurity, she solved my hesitation in yet another simple response that made all the sense in the world.

"Oh dearie, we'll just have to find someone to help you."

She could have told me I should have paid more attention in the freshman composition course we were all required to take in college. Or shamed me for having a master's degree, yet not feeling confident enough to write a book. She could have even pulled that religious card out of the deck and told me she would be praying for me, which usually means the only way you're going to succeed is with a miracle, and since those rarely occur, good luck! Instead, she almost matter-of-factly told me, "You can do this!" And I did, soon after releasing *Networking Is a Contact Sport*, which became a *New York Times* best-seller. Two brief but powerful statements from her, and I went from a confused and terrified rookie writer to a best-selling author.

How could anyone *not* fall in love with this nun?

When I first met Sister Camille, I was what some would call a "good Catholic." By that I mean I was a box checker. I went to Mass. I went to confession. I gave my money to the church. I performed all the rituals. To be honest, I didn't give a rat's ass about what all those boxes really meant. I did and said all the things I was supposed to do and say as a Catholic, believing that this is how you got to know God. I did all the right things not because I liked it, but because I felt I had to. It was from Sister Camille that I learned that knowing God isn't a head thing, but a faith that encompasses your entirety as a human being—body, mind, and soul. You pursued the things of God not because you *had* to, but because you *get* to. It changed my whole perspective on spiritual things and propelled me on a journey of discovering more of what I get to do rather than what I have to do. And being with her was maybe tops on that list. I never felt that I had to visit her or spend time with her. It was always, "Gee, I actually get to be with her today." Even with those cooler nuns in high school, I never felt that. What I really fell in love with was how to enjoy a deeper relationship with God and the divine.

So much of what I had experienced as a Catholic brought me up against rules. I swear they have a rule for everything. You go to Mass every Sunday. You don't eat meat on Fridays. You give something you like up for Lent. You don't use contraceptives. Sister Camille helped me see that rules in themselves are not all bad—that they form a container or vessel for us, which, especially when we are young, are necessary. But as we grow, our souls demand more space to grow and develop, yet whenever anyone tries to explore something new or different, the hierarchy consistently responds with, "No, we can't do that." Sister Camille was never like that. Her container was wide open. That's not to say she didn't believe the teachings of her faith. It's just that she was open to all of my questions—and I had plenty—never once telling me, "We can't do that," but always joining with me to see what we can learn from whatever source of inspiration and enlightenment I brought her. She truly believed that all knowledge comes from God, even knowledge that appears to contradict what we had been taught by our church.

I got gym time for the camp. but I got a whole lot more. That first encounter with Sister Camille began a process of blowing up the container that had been holding my fragile faith together. I had no idea what would take its place, and for the time being, I was more interested in getting my basketball camp going and building my career. But I couldn't get her out of my mind. Nor could I put my finger on what it was about her that captivated me so much. Knowing and connecting with Sister Camille, reminded me of Billy Joel's 1981 hit, "She's Got A Way."

This might have been the busiest time of my life up to that point. Kids. Work. Church. Friends. And the dreaded cocktail parties that seemed to graphically remind me how desperate I was to connect more deeply with the yearning that was rumbling deep within my soul. But how? It wasn't happening at the cocktail parties. Where could I turn to fill the emptiness that mathematician and philosopher René Descartes described as "the god-shaped hole" in my heart?

I was enamored with her presence and her being. There was something magnetic about her that I just couldn't escape.

— 4 —

A SACRED CONTRACT

As I did every morning, on that bright June day, I backed my car out onto our street and headed for the highway that took me to my office. Normally, I used my commute to mentally rehearse all I needed to do that day, worry about things like production schedules, challenging our sales team to find new clients– all those things that swirl around the brain of a young business owner.

Only on this commute, the farthest thing from my mind was my company.

As I headed down Calumet Road, instead of going straight I turned left onto Santa Monica Boulevard and, after a couple of more turns, found myself driving past Sister Camille's modest house that she shared with her sister, also a nun, Sister Joanne Marie. I'm not a guy who likes to waste a lot of time, but here I was, instead of taking the fastest and most direct route to my office, I took a slight detour that allowed me to drive through Sister Camille's neighborhood. And here's the part I need to explain carefully: I secretly hoped I'd see her out in the yard.

That may sound a bit strange to you. A hard-charging businessman in his forties going out of his way to connect with a nun who was quickly becoming a trusted confidant, friend, and mentor. And to be honest, I surprised myself. I mean, I thought we were so different, but after some reflection, I realized we were more alike than different. Sister was, in her own right, a strong businesswoman and leader in the Milwaukee community. She was the first female president of the Rotary Club of Milwaukee, and gained tremendous respect by business leaders in the community that she networked with as President of Cardinal Stritch to advance the institution's mission. She could dine with kings and royalty but had the touch of a common woman with incredible business acumen. Maybe this relationship wasn't so illogical after all. My soul was parched, and this dear, godly woman seemed to know where I could find what I was looking for: meaning, purpose, fulfillment, joy, and most important, connection to something bigger and more magnificent than my current understanding of life as I knew it.

At the time, I probably couldn't have explained why I was so connected to this quaint, old, Catholic nun, which is why I keep going back to her magnetic attraction. If you place a handful of nuts and bolts on a table next to a powerful magnet, they immediately slide straight to the magnet. I was one of those nuts, and Sister was a powerful magnet. We had no formal relationship, but going a little out of my way seemed a small price to pay for maybe getting a chance to spend some time with her, which I did.

At first, I leaned on the idea that I was only stopping by to help an older woman out with things she couldn't possibly do by herself. Right! Like she couldn't possibly walk out on the sidewalk and retrieve her newspaper, one of those tasks I assigned myself? She may have been old, but she was perfectly capable of hard work. One beastly hot day in August, I pulled into her driveway and knocked on her door. I heard her call me to come in and when I walked into her kitchen she was scrubbing the linoleum floor. Sister Camille did not need me as much as I needed her. Sure, I helped with things like raking her lawn, shoveling snow from her sidewalk, and trimming her shrubs, but the truth is, those were just excuses to be able to spend time with her, which always became invigorating and insightful conversations that sent me on my way more energized than I had ever felt when I left business meetings or even church on Sunday.

For example, one time I stopped by, ostensibly to shovel her sidewalks. It was a gloomy December morning, and I honestly was concerned that she might slip and fall if I didn't clear her walk and the driveway. But sure enough, she appeared at the door and motioned for me to come in, which I did. But instead of small talk, she looked me right in the eyes and asked, "How are things going with your company?" First of all, in all the many cocktail parties and other social events I attended, no one ever asked me that. Instead, us guys talked about the Bucks and the Brewers, which is great for about five minutes. But for three hours? Second, I could tell that Sister wasn't just making conversation. She asked with an earnestness that told me she really cared.

"Sister, I've got to be honest," I began. "Some days I wonder if it's all worth it. I mean between raising four kids and trying to keep my business growing, I barely have time to think."

Even as I said that I thought to myself, "What am I doing? She's got a university to run. Why am I bothering this lovely old nun with my problems?"

I felt as if I was taking unfair advantage of our nascent friendship. Until she answered.

"Why Joe, maybe you need to give yourself the gift of time just to think and reflect."

"Well that's great advice, Sister. But what do you do?"

"Well dearie, in my life sometimes things get crazy at Cardinal Stritch. So, I have learned to bookend my days with rituals."

"What do you mean by that, Sister? Bookending your days?"

"I realized that if I created sacred times when I wake up and just before I go to bed, I can handle whatever comes at me during the day."

In my typical time sensitive fashion, I asked "How long does this take?"

"Well dearie. It lasts until I am ready to say yes to the day."

I've since hired business coaches and consultants, but none spoke words that I needed to hear more than those. She had the amazing ability to cut through all the verbiage that comprises most conversations and get right to what I needed to hear. As I reflect back on it, her counsel seems so obvious as to be almost simplistic. But it was exactly what I needed. I thought, like most men, that it's somehow honorable to be busy, but my busyness was draining my soul. My company was getting ahead, my kids were doing fine, but even on a good day, I felt as if I was chained to a treadmill that didn't have a pause button. So much of what people say to each other seems to be part of an endless competition to impress each other.

"We just found out that Tim got into Notre Dame."

"I never thought I'd say this, but I like my Lexus better than our Mercedes."

"Why don't you join us in our suite at Fiserv?"

"We'd love to, but we're taking the kids to Vail over the holidays."

I have nothing against nice cars and fun vacations, but I had reached a point where talking about these things just didn't do it for me. These are first-world, rich people problems. And like most people in my social circle, I was working my tail off to be able to do all those things, but talking about them endlessly left me feeling empty, almost to the point of panic.

When Sister spoke, it was as if she could see inside my soul. No one had ever given me permission to just sit and think. If I ever complained about being too busy, which we all sort of do just to impress each other, the usual response is something like, "Sounds like you need a vacation," which usually meant more stress, more work, more busyness, only to return from your vacation more exhausted than when you left. I really did need to give myself the gift of some time to just sit and think, and somehow Sister Camille knew that. What an incredible mentor she had become.

It was during this period of my sort of planned "accidental" meetings that I began to sense that I could be completely honest around her, especially when it came to the issue of spirituality. That may sound odd, but most of my adult Catholic life I felt like a bit of an imposter. By that I mean I had lots of questions about certain religious and spiritual teachings but felt as if I had to keep them to myself. I would go to Mass and attend other church functions and hear things that made me really scratch my head, but I would nod and smile like everyone else because that's sort of what was expected of you.

For example, around this time I discovered and began reading the writings of Father Richard Rohr, a Catholic priest who some in the church view as wandering outside the lines of Catholic orthodoxy. By his own admission, he has been heavily influenced by Buddhism, Hinduism, the teachings of Gandhi, Carl Jung, and the distinctly non-religious theories of Spiral Dynamics. Frankly, Rohr's views made a lot more sense to me than a lot of what I had been taught in catechism, but I knew enough to keep my thoughts on him to myself. Deep down inside, I yearned to be able to explore his ideas with someone without the fear of being rejected.

It was with a tiny bit of nervousness that I mentioned Fr. Rohr, a fellow Franciscan, to Sister Camille. After all, I didn't want to spoil what was becoming a highly valued friendship by confessing my growing interest in a guy somewhat on the outs with many Catholic leaders. I was only slightly surprised, yet wonderfully relieved, to learn that she not only did not consider him to be a heretic but resonated with a lot of what he wrote. And wasn't afraid to admit that to me.

"Remember Joe, if it's true, God must be in it, and I see a lot of truth in what he writes."

This somewhat casual relationship continued for about five or six years, and to be clear, we did not often dig deep into matters of the soul or spirituality. In a way, I didn't need to, for just being with her gave me a rush. She could show me the birds hovering around her bird feeder or point out a favorite plant in her flower garden, and that was enough for me. Most of the time, I would only be with her for twenty or thirty minutes, but I always left feeling energized and optimistic, regardless of what awaited me at work. In a very real way, I was falling in love, but not in a romantic way. The Greeks had four different words for love: agape (love for God); storge (love among parents and children); eros (romantic or intimate love); and philia (affectionate, friendship, a virtuous love). Our culture has become so addicted to eros that mentioning you love someone often leaves the wrong impression. When I say I was falling in love, I was literally falling into a genuine, authentic, and virtuous friendship with another human being who expected nothing of me other than to be myself.

We even discussed the topic of intimacy. People think that intimacy is about sex, but it's really about truth. When you realize you can tell someone your truth, when you can show yourself to them, when you stand in front of them with all the good, bad, and ugly exposed and the response is "you're safe with me," that's intimacy. That's what I felt with Sister Camille.

A few years ago, I read a remarkable book: *Sacred Contracts,* by Caroline Myss. It had such an impact on me that I reread it. Three times. And have written and underlined nearly every sentence in it. One of the many things I learned from this author are the two most important questions facing us as we negotiate our way through life: 1. Where am I going? And 2. Who will go with me? Once we know the answers to these questions, we are able to determine our "sacred contract," which she defines as our higher purpose. By the time I met Sister Camille, I had pretty much figured out the answer to the first one. I am an entrepreneur. A business owner. A leader. I enjoy helping others figure out how to become the best versions of themselves, and I have found a way to combine those into a somewhat successful career. The second question, in my opinion, has to do with who we discover to mentor us through the challenges of life. For some, it may be a spouse, but for most people, that trustworthy guide lies elsewhere, and our job is to find that person and connect with him or her. I honestly believe that my need for a gym was orchestrated by a higher source of energy that is available to all of us. And in future chapters I hope to help you discover how to tap into that energy in order to find your own Sister Camille. In any event, I believe that I was predestined to meet Sister Camille, not just as a provider of a gym or an interesting friend, but as someone who would be a reliable mentor for my journey on earth and beyond.

So now that we are perfectly clear about the kind of love I was falling into, maybe you can understand why I refer to these years of casual meetings as something of a courtship. The more I was with her, the better I felt. And almost as soon as I drove away to get to my office, I longed to see her again.

I also sensed that she had similar feelings toward me. I mean it's not like she ever brushed me off and said she was busy or had to get to her office. We liked each other, but it was more than that. Our relationship grew into a pure and holy kind of love, but what does that mean? I'm not sure where I read this, but it describes the kind of love we shared: "To really love someone is to be the silent guardian of another person's solitude." That's what we did for each other. A seventy-something year old nun and a forty-something business owner and man searching for a deeper meaning in life.

And then her sister died.

Sister Camille and her sister Joanne were extremely close, and both were remarkable women who served God through the Sisters of St. Francis of Assisi. Sister Joanne had a passion for children and founded the St. Francis Children's Center, just off the campus of Cardinal Stritch University, to provide educational opportunities for children with special needs. Ironically, she began the center with the help of a Jewish businessman, a testament to how both sisters drew their theological circles wide to include many.

Naturally, I went to Sister Joanne's funeral mass and offered my condolences to my friend Sister Camille.

"Please, Sister, if there's anything you need, please let me know."

A few weeks passed when my phone rang.

"Joe, this is Sister Camille. I have to attend a fundraiser for Catholic schools. In the past, my sister always accompanied me, but of course, she's gone. I need a date. Would you mind going with me?

Would I? I felt like I just won the lottery. Of course, I would.

At the appointed date, I put on my best suit and drove over to Sister Camille's house to pick her up. I've sat through my share of fundraisers, usually fighting to stay awake, but this one was different. Same chicken dinner. Same cheap wine. And same plea to keep the schools open. Only this time, I had the time of my life. It was just so much fun to be with her, yet I can't for the life of me remember what we talked about. What I do remember is that we laughed a lot, which made me feel as if maybe I was able to offer her a little joy in the aftermath of losing her sister.

That was the turning point—the moment we both realized that our friendship was neither accidental or casual. We had become best friends. Could we be soulmates? It was meant to be. Not in a tawdry or irreverent manner, but almost a divine connection that transcends family, gender, financial status, even faith. Thanks to Facebook, the term friendship has been reduced to whoever clicks the right box on a screen. I know people who have thousands of friends on Facebook, and I truly hope those friendships are fulfilling, but I suspect in many cases, they don't even know most of those friends. Wherever I've lived, I, too, have had many friends, but only a precious few that I would call close.

After I dropped Sister Camille off at her house following a full evening at the fundraiser, it dawned on me. This is pretty serious. It's also pretty awesome. I just spent a delightful evening with a great woman of faith who is building a tremendous university and who seems to value our connection as much as I do. What could be better than that?

I was about to find out.

— 5 —

ENTERING THE CONFESSIONAL

For several years, my relationship with this elderly nun could best be described as casual. I would stop by her house, ostensibly to help her with something, but really just to get a chance to talk a bit. Or we would run into each other at a social or church function and somehow always ended up chatting for more than the polite (and shallow) minute or two. She knew I represented several Packers including MVP, Brett Favre, and being a fanatical Packers fan—something of a redundancy—always liked to hear a story or two about one of her favorite Packers. Or I might ask her about some special project she had initiated at the university and even though it was her job to raise money, she never hit me up for a donation. That was kind of big for me because in my experience as a business owner, it seemed that the big shots at church or other non-profits only came by when they wanted a check.

Whenever and wherever we met, space opened up, and we could talk about anything. Sometimes our discussions gravitated toward the church. Ever since I was fifteen, I have been questioning spirituality and the church. And in that process, I had begun to explore some ideas that some would feel ran counter to the teachings of the church, and even though I had sensed a much more open, generous attitude from Sister Camille toward other religions, I so enjoyed just being with her that I didn't want to risk offending her or creating a barrier between us. Trust me, I knew what it was like to be called out for thinking outside the four walls of my church.

In my last book, *After Further Review,* I had shared briefly how some of the teachings of Buddhism, Taoism, and other Eastern religions not only made sense to me but were helpful as I attempted to negotiate the challenges of life. One evening, I found myself again at one of those social obligations that always seem to pop up, and if you're at all involved in the civic life of your city or community, you know exactly what I'm talking about. Anyway, I was doing my best to be sociable when an acquaintance approached me, perhaps a little emboldened by her glass of wine (or maybe three).

"Hey Joe," she began. "I read your latest book. What the hell are you? A Buddhist? A goddam Hindu? For Chrissake I thought you were a Catholic, but it looks to me like you're actually buying all that bullshit from those foreigners!"

I don't recall if I prayed for grace or patience or restraint because all I said was, "It's been nice," and walked away. I'm not real proud of my rudeness, but it was a whole lot better than saying what I *really* wanted to say to her. As I walked away, I wish I would have handled it better and remembered what Cardinal Dolan, one of my favorite people, said he does when people attack him. This is a man who has been under attack for the sexual abuse scandal in the Catholic Church, so his words carried incredible wisdom for me. He does four things:

1. He acknowledges their concerns and admits wrongdoing. "We made mistakes."

2. He personalizes it. "It makes me sick too."

3. He tries to give a perspective on it. "As a church, we do millions of incredible things. Many good deeds. We've had some bad apples, and there is no excuse for that. I wish we would have handled it better."

4. He closes with humor. When recently grilled by a reporter for stating he would have loved to have a wife and child, he leaned in and nonchalantly asked the reporter was she doing for dinner that night, as only Cardinal Dolan can do.

The last thing I wanted was to offend Sister Camille or make her uncomfortable by bringing up some of the very real and honest questions I was having about spiritual matters. At the same time, I had come to respect her so much that I felt it would be dishonest of me not to share what was going on in my life; what really mattered to me. I also sensed from her generous spirit that if she indeed felt I was crossing the line theologically or careening off into perdition, she would very gently and kindly tell me as much. I just didn't want to let her down.

On occasion, I would call her office and ask she if she had some time to meet with me, being careful not to abuse that privilege. Almost always she made time for me and when the weather permitted, we would walk across the visitor's parking lot and sit on a bench beneath a grove of young maple trees. So, it was that we found ourselves on that bench one sunny spring day, but instead of my usual anticipation at seeing her, I was nervous as hell. It was almost as if I was going to confession, but instead of making up some little innocuous sins to keep the priest at bay for another year, I was about to confess my alternative views of church and religion. At least that's what I thought.

I had just finished reading a remarkable book, *Wishes Fulfilled,* by Dr. Wayne Dyer, and it's not an exaggeration to say it had a life-changing effect on me. In fact, I consider him to be one of the best spiritual teachers to have come along in the past fifty years. He just made so much sense to me. Yet I knew that in some circles—especially among conservative Christians—he's considered to be off limits, and that's putting it mildly. I brought the book with me really as a way to stick my toe in the water to see if she approved of him or not. But I was also sincerely hoping to ask her some questions about some of the things Dyer wrote about. Imagine my relief when she saw the book and exclaimed, "I see you're reading Wayne Dyer. I love what he's doing."

I remember thinking, this woman not only gets Wayne Dyer, she gets *me.* Any time I mentioned to some of my friends or colleagues the books I was reading or the ideas I was exploring, they would look at me like I had just arrived from another planet. They would either laugh off my interest in those "whacky ideas" or condemn me to hell for wandering off the true path to God, which, according to them, was the Catholic church. Here was a prominent leader in that church affirming my curiosity in a guy whose writing was so helpful to me. Thrilled but still a little apprehensive, I pressed her on one of Dyer's teachings that I had never heard before but seemed so comforting if not entirely plausible.

"Sister, if I'm reading him correctly, Dyer believes that we can never be separated from God. That seems to contradict everything I've been taught about God. I'd love to know what you think about that."

Like a lot of people, I had this vision of God being way off somewhere sitting on a big throne, and to get close to him or accepted by him I had to follow all these rules and perform all sorts of rituals and duties, and maybe if I was lucky, he would give me a little pat on the head like some cosmic grandad. Dyer basically calls that view of God the biggest lie ever, explaining that we are never separated from God. Ever. When I read that, it gave me so much hope and even confirmed my own experience with a kind of divine energy that was always within reach. According to Dyer, I didn't have to do anything to enjoy God's presence. He or she was always there with me. I didn't have to wait long for Sister's answer.

"Why dearie, of course we are never separated from God. He's always with us, even when we reject him. If he seems distant or even absent, it's because we've pushed him away or ignored him. Yet he's still there, always on our side, always pulling for us. But don't take my word for it. The great apostle, St. Paul, wrote that 'neither death, nor life, nor angels, nor principalities, nor powers, nor things present, nor things to come, nor height, nor depth, nor any other creature, shall be able to separate us from the love of God.'"

I could have hugged her, but the students walking by on their way to class might have thought it was a little weird to see the president of their university getting hugged by a guy a lot younger than her. I would learn later that one reason she had such appreciation for Dyer is that both found ways to combine religion, spirituality, and psychology.

How could you not love this woman—a truly modern day saint?

That sort of opened the floodgates. When I expressed surprise that she not only was familiar with Dyer and others but agreed with a lot of what he had to say, she reminded me that she studied psychology as an undergraduate and in graduate school. Dyer also studied psychology and at one time served as professor of psychology at St. John's University, another Catholic school, albeit a much larger one than Cardinal Stritch. I, too, earned a degree in industrial psychology, so I decided to push a little further and ask about one of my favorite psychologists and authors. Viktor Frankl. Frankl, as you probably know, was a Holocaust survivor and largely based on his experiences in four Nazi death camps, including Auschwitz, wrote *Man's Search for Meaning*. At one time, according to the Library of Congress, it was considered to be one of the ten most influential books in the United States. It certainly had influenced me. I've read it several times and have underlined most of it and written copious notes in the margins. Although it is a deeply spiritual book, Frankl was not particularly religious, certainly not a Catholic. But once again, when I threw him into our conversation, Sister never flinched.

"I love that book, dearie. Especially the part where he writes about love between people existing even after one has died. You know his beloved wife died in a concentration camp, and he never lost his connection to her."

I couldn't believe it. That was one of my favorite passages in my marked up little book:

Love goes very far beyond the physical person of the beloved. It finds its deepest meaning in his or her spiritual being, in his or her inner self. Whether or not he or she is actually present, whether or not he or she is still alive at all, ceases somehow to be of importance.

I asked her what she thought that meant, and she explained that what Frankl is really talking about is the soul. How the purest form of love lasts forever and is not confined to place or time. For her, this gave her great comfort when her sister died, and she regularly talked with her sister. I thought, what the hell, I might as well go for it.

"Sister, maybe you think I'm crazy, but I've formed a virtual board of directors that I reach out to for guidance, and many who are on my board have passed. People like Ronald Reagan, Thomas Merton, Thomas Edison, St. Ignatius of Loyola and St. Francis of Assisi. They may not be present on this earth, but I consult them on a regular basis."

"Oh no, dearie, you're not crazy at all. In fact, I have my own virtual board of directors, primarily saints. St. Teresa of Ávila, Saint Teresa of Calcutta, St. Clare, as well as many others. Our souls live on forever. Even though Joanne is no longer physically present, she is very much present, and I talk to her all the time."

Finally, I thought to myself, here's someone who doesn't think I'm a nutcase. All my life I'd been taught that we've got all these religions at odds with each other. The Protestants were over in one corner of the room. The Catholics in another. The Jews were way over there someplace, and the Muslims, Hindus, Buddhists, and others weren't even allowed in the house. And here I was sitting on a bench at a Catholic university with a nun who also happens to be president of that university, and she's praising the ideas of a Jewish guy who was very likely an agnostic who acknowledged in an interview that he believes in a deity that he calls "super-meaning, a meaning so comprehensive that you can no longer grasp it."

Every now and then a student passing by would wave or call out to Sister, and she always answered back, often addressing them by their names. It dawned on me that this humble nun was the perfect person to lead a university that served not only Catholics, but students of all religions or no religion. There was a wideness in her understanding of God that could embrace not only all of her students, but a hard-charging business owner trying to understand what to do with ideas that inspired me so much but that were considered to be outside the box I had lived in for so long.

"Always remember, dearie. If it helps you become a better person, if it brings you joy and meaning, it must be from God."

By now I was like a little kid on the edge of his seat waiting for the teacher to give me a treat, but of course, I maintained my adult composure, trying my best to keep up with her assessment of these great thinkers. I came to this meeting somewhat fearful that I was about to out myself as a heretic, but so far, she did not bring out a ruler and smack my hands. I pressed on.

"Sister, we both studied psychology, what do you think of the psychologist, Carl Jung."

I didn't tell her I was a huge fan of Jung's and found his concept of synchronicity to make more sense than anything I had learned in church. Here is a psychologist that, better than anyone, connected psychology and spirituality. Basically, he explained that people and events don't just show up. We're in a vibrational flow of energy where we connect with people who vibrate in the same place that we are. I tried to explain that to a friend once, and he asked me if I was getting enough potassium in my diet. Sister Camille had a different take on that.

"Oh dearie, I've read most everything Jung has written, and I believe his concept of synchronicity explains our friendship. Think of it. We really come from two different worlds, yet here we are, sitting on a bench talking about things that we both love. Do you honestly think this just happened? Of course, you don't!"

I could hardly believe what I was hearing, but I liked it, and it gave me courage to jump in even deeper. Against my better judgement, I asked her what she thought of Joseph Campbell, another author I had read and whose ideas I found so helpful. Basically, Campbell explains all belief systems in terms of myth that are all part of one great story that he calls monomyth. To him, "God is a metaphor for a mystery that transcends all categories of human thought, even the categories of being and non-being." Toward the end of his book *Transformations of Myth Through Time*, Campbell said that all the ancient religions were outdated, archaic, no longer capable of speaking to us and dangerous. Needless to say, you don't hear many priests or preachers quoting Joseph Campbell in their homilies.

"I'll have to admit some people think that he's pretty far out there sometimes," Sister Camille responded when I brought him into our conversation. "But a lot of what he says rings true. I've always believed that all knowledge comes from God; we can't dismiss something just because it comes from someone we don't always agree with."

We had been talking for just under an hour, and I always tried to be mindful of her time. She had a university to run; I had a business and family to care for. It's that whole you-don't-want-to-wear-out-your-welcome thing, but to Sister's credit, she never looked at her watch or seemed in a hurry whenever we met. In my world, everyone's in a hurry to get who knows where, and then in a bigger hurry to leave. Sister Camille was never like that, which made it so refreshing to spend time with her. One of the things I learned from her was to always appreciate the now. She always lived in the present, which is kind of what a saint does. She wasn't worried about the next meeting, instead, she lived for the present. She had that rare quality of making you feel like you were the most important person to her. But as it turned out, this really was a watershed moment in our relationship. I had scheduled this time to test the waters. To see if what was going on in my inner life had any validity to someone like Sister. My quest for answers to the big questions of life made me feel like I didn't fit in. An outsider. I would go to Mass and walk out thinking, "What's wrong with me?" I would attend social events and listen to what everyone else was talking about and think, "Am I just a big whackadoodle for not giving two shits about any of this stuff?" Like all of us, I wanted to fit in, to be accepted. I wasn't intentionally trying to make people uncomfortable or angry. I just seemed to be on another wavelength, and hardly anyone else was interested in joining me there. My great fear was that if I was completely honest with Sister Camille, she would confirm my sense of being out of sync with what is right and true. In a way, that's exactly what she did, but in such a generous manner that not only affirmed me but gave me hope and inspiration.

"Oh dearie," she chuckled when I shared my fear of being a misfit. "You don't fit in, and that's perfectly fine. I still love you, and God does too."

Well she didn't straight up call me a whackadoodle, and since I was in good company, I felt pretty damn good.

6

REFRAMING THE IMAGE OF GOD
(IS OUR GOD TOO SMALL?)

When it comes to God, you could call me a "closet seeker." I had been taught that there was only one god, and his name was, well, God. But I had developed an enormous curiosity about all those other gods and deities like Buddha, Lao Tzu, and the many Hindu deities– such as Krishna and Kali. If there really is only one god, then who are these? Are they, as I had been taught, "false gods," or could they in some way be connected to each other?

After that exhilarating conversation with Sister Camille about so-called progressive thinkers like Richard Rohr and Joseph Campbell, I practically walked on air for the next several days. She not only made me feel as if it was okay to engage ideas that challenged some of what I had been taught, she encouraged it. She seemed so secure in what she believed that new ways of looking at things didn't threaten her, didn't elicit an automatic defense of her beloved Church's teaching. I was so hungry for more, but at the same time I didn't want to press my luck. It's one thing to read a few books that challenged some Christian teachings; I was having some serious questions about God himself/herself/itself. What would Sister Camille think of me for going after the Big Guy?

When we met the next time, I had already decided to go for it, though I started out with a fairly safe question. As before, I met her at her office, and we walked across the parking lot to that little grove of maples and sat down together on the park bench.

"Well dearie," she began. "What would you like to talk about today?"

One of the many things I loved about Sister Camille is that she always seemed genuinely interested in me. I had noticed that when others were with us—she had a way of making everyone around her feel as if they were the most important person in the world. I don't think she was just being polite; I honestly believed that this was part of her faith. Even though I'm no biblical scholar, I know that it says a lot about putting others first, and that's exactly how Sister lived.

"Well Sister, let's talk about God."

"Oh my," she laughed. "We could be here all day! Where should we start?"

And that's another thing—I never saw Sister look at her watch during our many times together. You got the feeling that if it would take an entire day for her to answer my question, she would do it. My entire professional life at the time was heavily scheduled with meetings, appointments, conference calls, and the like. Almost as soon as I got into a meeting, I started glancing at my watch, thinking about my next appointment. I've learned from her to live more in the moment, to slow down and savor even the smallest of gifts that come our way, such as the rabbits, deer, chipmunks, squirrels, foxes, and wild turkeys that show up in my yard every evening. My apprehension about sharing my doubts and questions about God with Sister began to evaporate.

"Sister, I know that you believe that there's only one true god, and that his name is God. But what about all those deities from other religions? For example, when one of my Japanese businessmen friends prays to Buddha, is he praying to the same god we're all praying to.?"

"Why that's a wonderful question and an important one. And you're right, I do believe that there's only one true God. For me, that's the God we learn about from the Bible, or a book that Sister Camille referred to as basic instruction before leaving earth. When it comes to Buddha or any other deity for that matter, I'm not real sure. What do you think?"

One of the things that has always bugged me about conservative Christians is that they're all so damn certain that they're right. Here was a woman of deep Christian faith admitting that she didn't know everything about God or her beloved religion. I loved that.

Sister said, "Dearie, I don't really like talking about religion because when people talk about religion, they always want to argue about who is right. On the other hand, when people talk about spirituality, they just want to know about one thing: How do I get more of it?"

"Sister, it seems like all spiritual people desire some kind of connection with a divine being. So, what if we quit using the name of God for a hundred years? What do you think would happen?"

"Oh dearie, I'm going to have to think about that one, and maybe you can help me by telling me what you have in mind."

That was so like her. I could tell that my question posed a challenge to her. I mean, God had been God to her for her entire life, and now I come along and try to change his name. Or at least her perception of God. But instead of telling me I was nuts or worse, a heretic, she took my question seriously, which was so affirming to me. Up until this point, I never felt I could talk about this with anyone, certainly not with any of my priests or teachers. I've met so many Catholic and Protestant Christians that didn't take kindly to serious questions about God, which is really a shame because genuine spirituality ought to not just be comfortable with questions but encourage them.

I began to unpack all that was rumbling around in my soul about God or whomever, and she patiently listened.

As far as Sister was concerned, the name "God" is too confining. Too limiting. It assumes that the deity that goes by that name is limited to Christianity, primarily, and possibly Judaism, though Jews believe the name is so holy that they do not write it out fully. To them, God is G-d. I also have a problem referring to God as "Father" because it gives the impression that "he" is sort of like us, only bigger and more powerful. Perhaps "humanizing" God—what really smart people call anthropomorphism—helps some people get their arms around him, so to speak. But it also, in Sister's opinion, diminishes our concept of what God is really like. Is God really a man? A woman? Does he have a long, white beard? Does she wear a white robe? Does this deity speak, and if so, in what language? Is God a being that we can see? According to the Old Testament, Moses asked to see God, but he never really saw him face-to-face (Exodus 33:19-33).

"Sister, have you?"

"Yes, I see God every day, in the students, my teachers, the birds in the sky, and the rabbits running around the university."

Then there's that big question about other religions. Each has a deity; some have many. Are they any more or less of a god than God? According to the monotheistic religions (Christianity, Judaism, and Islam), there's only one true god. But which is it: God, Jehovah, or Allah? And isn't it more than a little arrogant to say that my god is the real one and yours isn't? Yet that's what these religions teach. Ironically, they've been at each other's throats for centuries, often fighting wars over who's got the right god.

I recently discovered a book written in 1953 by a modern Bible translator. Its title expresses exactly the same sentiment I feel about how most people think about God: *Your God Is Too Small.* While I don't entirely agree with everything in this book, I can relate to his overall premise that we cannot fully understand God because we have made him in our own image. In other words, God is just like us, only a little stronger, a little smarter, sometimes really loving and kind, other times mean and punitive. That's the image of God most of us have been taught, yet it doesn't come close to describing this divine being that I believe is always with us.

How about we just change the name? Better yet, why don't we try to come up with a more accurate image to illustrate this force or power—this deity—that we call God?

Some of you might remember how in the first "Star Wars" movie, Obi-Wan Kenobi frequently offered these words to his friends and allies: "May the Force be with you." It was often used when people were leaving each other to face a significant or dangerous challenge. It was almost a prayer or benediction in which Obi-Wan was asking a supernatural power to be with that person. Notably, the Force was not a god as we think of deity, but more a source of energy available to whoever sought it.

What if we replaced the word God with energy?

That makes so much more sense to me. What we think of as God is really a universal energy that flows through all of us, primarily through nature, in loving another person, or in experiences. I know of many people who seldom or never go to church and who say things like, "My church is the forest," or "When I take my morning run on the beach, I feel the closest to God." I know exactly what they mean. One time I gave myself a spiritual retreat, spending a weekend pretty much alone in a sparse cabin. There were no icons or stained glass, no one reading prayers, and no pipe organ accompanying hymns. Yet I was practically lifted off my feet by this powerful energy that seemed to flow through me. I heard and saw things with such clarity—the song of the birds outside my door, the sunlight flooding my room. I even watched a spider for more than an hour, filled with wonder and amazement is it weaved its intricate web. All of that was God—a force field of energy available to everyone, anytime. There's no beginning, no end. It permeates the universe yet lies within reach of all. You don't need to follow specific man-made rules to gain access to this energy. You don't have to belong to a particular religion or practice any religion at all. As I was sharing all of this with Sister Camille, I could see that she was thinking really hard, paying close attention to every word. When I finally finished trying to describe what I really thought about God, she sat there for a moment, looking off into the cloudless sky, a slight breeze tugging at the habit she always wore. I wondered if maybe I had gone too far, and she was looking for the right words to gently correct me.

"I'm not convinced we need to change his name, but I think your concept of God makes sense. It's kind of like those cute little rabbits that show up around here all the time. The same life force that makes their hearts beat, makes mine beat as well. Isn't that the energy you're talking about? Well, I happen to call that God, but I think we're speaking of the same thing."

Once again, I was blown away, not only by her openness to new ideas, but by her wisdom. She wasn't backing away from the name for the God she loved and had served all her adult life, but it was clear that she shared an image of God that was not confined or limited by our tendency to put God in a little box that sits in the closet until we need him. She explained that our practice of giving God human characteristics at first makes him seem accessible, but eventually turns him into a cosmic Santa Claus or good luck charm.

"I like your idea of a force, dearie, because I've always felt that our relationship with God is more of a connection to something that is always there, always with us. He's so much more than someone we experience one day a week in a cathedral or go to whenever we're in trouble"

And then she flashed that mischievous smile and added, "But if you don't mind, I'll still call him God."

Now we were both laughing. Who was I to tell Sister Camille what to do? I was just so thrilled that she didn't think I was crazy. That's not to say she was done with me.

"Now back to your comments about Buddha. You seem to think there are similarities between the Buddha and Jesus. Tell me more."

I explained that I had read that despite the fact that Buddha lived 600 years before Jesus and they were separated by around 3,000 miles, they shared re-markably similar stories and taught similar truths. As the book *Jesus and Buddha* by Marcus Borg and Jack Kornfield explained, both were conceived in a way that is considered miraculous. Their mothers' names were similar (Maya for Buddha, Mary for Jesus). They both faced a period of temptation by the devil, began a traveling ministry in their thirties, performed miracles, and renounced wealth and luxury.

Sister politely listened and without making me feel foolish, revealed that she was quite familiar with Buddha and Buddhism.

"As you probably also know, dearie, Jesus taught a lot of things that Buddha had taught, and there's no evidence that Jesus was aware of that. Both taught that we are to love our enemies, turn the other cheek when we are wronged, help those in need, and share our faith with others. I'm not sure that necessarily means Buddha and Jesus are the same deity."

"Okay, maybe they aren't really the same person, but what if God really *is* this force of positive energy and the various deities that mankind has worshiped from the beginning are connected to that source? Couldn't their teachings and their examples come from that energy?"

"That's certainly a possibility, dearie. You know, of course, that we like to say that with God, all things are possible. I'm not going to say you're wrong. And if your theory is true, it wouldn't change anything for me because I believe that in some mysterious way, we're all connected to God. He is always present; we can never be separated from him. If we sometimes feel as if he's absent, it's because we've chosen to ignore him. But he's always there, and we're always connected. If your Japanese friend connects to God through Buddha, that's wonderful!"

How could I not love this wise little nun? She made me feel so comfortable raising these questions, and instead of trying to correct me, she did something that few of us do anymore: she listened. Really listened to what some thought was sacrilege, acknowledging that she didn't have all the answers and that mine weren't so far out. Her openness to new ideas emboldened me to tackle another "sacred cow" that was especially relevant that day, the Feast of the Holy Trinity. Trinity Sunday is the first Sunday after Pentecost in Western Christian Liturgical calendars. Trinity Sunday celebrates the Christian doctrine of the Trinity, something I have never been able to get my arms around. Now might be my chance to get Sister's perspective on this.

Ever since I was a kid, the whole "three in one" thing seemed like a bunch of spiritual mumbo-jumbo. Don't take my word for it. Consider this from the Catechism of the Catholic Church:

> What is the Blessed Trinity? The Blessed Trinity means that in the one God there are three distinct and equal Persons: the Father, the Son, and the Holy Spirit. What do we mean by the equality and distinction of the divine Persons? The three divine Persons are perfectly equal to one another because all are the one and infinitely perfect God. The three divine Persons are really distinct from one another. They are not three names for the same Person, nor are the three Persons blended into one another. This means: The Father is not the Son. The Son is not the Holy Spirit. The Father is not the Holy Spirit.

Huh?

That was my honest reaction to the Church's teaching about the Trinity. I wasn't trying then, nor am I now, to be disrespectful. It just didn't make sense, and no amount of explaining cleared things up for me. Three distinct persons, but yet they're equal. How does that work, and which one do I go to when I pray? And is God really a person? I could tell that this was really important to a lot of people, and it seemed like they accepted it without question, so I just kept my thoughts to myself, figuring that someday it might make sense to me. Today was that day.

"Sister, I need to also tell you that I have a big problem with the Trinity—the whole Father, Son, and Holy Spirit. It just doesn't make any sense to me."

"Oh dearie, there are a lot of things in the Bible that don't make sense to me, but that's where faith comes in. It's the gift of believing things we can't prove; can't see."

I had heard that most of my life, and I agree that there's a lot about spirituality that you can't see, but it always seemed like a cop out—a respectable answer when you really didn't have one. I pressed on.

"It's not that I don't believe in the Trinity, Sister. I just see it a little differently."

I reached into my pocket and pulled out a little notebook and drew a triangle. At the bottom left angle, I scratched the letter C for Camille. Over to the other angle at the bottom of the triangle, I wrote J, for Joe. Then at the top, I wrote the words energy and God.

"When I think of the Trinity, Sister, I think about when two people connect and do all this neat stuff together and find themselves shifting from the 'me' to the 'we.' That's the union of two souls. But then they sense this desire to reach out, and that's the calling. Who's doing the calling? The creator, or what I prefer to call the Divine Energy. Real trinity begins with union with another person that connects to the energy of the creator or divine force, but it doesn't stay with that triangle. It always flows outward, sharing that divine energy with others. Our mission, then, is to take the energy from the Trinity and share it with others. So right now, Sister, *we* are the Trinity—an energy field from above flowing through us and then shared outwardly with others."

Once again, she listened carefully, and after I finished, remained silent for a few moments. Even in that silence, I could feel a powerful energy flowing through every cell of my body.

"I really like your idea of tapping into energy and then sharing it with others," she began. She paused for a moment, and I could see by that scrunched up look on her face that she was thinking really hard, choosing her words carefully. She took the little piece of paper with my sketches on it, pointed to the top of the little triangle, and continued.

"But you know, dearie, this could still be the Father, and over here it's the Son, and over on the left is the Holy Spirit. And yes, we can all tap into this divine Trinity that gives us the power and motivation to reach out to others."

But sister, that's a head thing—too impersonal. I don't think you can understand the Trinity unless you experience it. This connection is about a union of two people like you and me—the union of two doesn't absorb distinction but actually intensifies it. The more one gives in the creative union to another the more we become one self and connect with the higher power.

In her sweet and respectful way, she was essentially telling me that she didn't totally agree with me, but at the same time, she wasn't criticizing me or shaming me. She didn't tell me I was dangerously tampering with the truth. I had just rearranged one of the most cherished doctrines of her faith, and yet she made me feel as if my ideas were legitimate and were worthy of serious consideration, and in doing so, she affirmed my value as a person.

I've never had a problem with religion or spiritual movements that believe what they teach is right. It's the predictable next move they often make that bothers me: we're right, so you must be wrong. It's that black and white approach to spirituality that has created such a wide divide between the world's great religions, even leading them to wage wars against each other. Even within Christianity, where everyone pretty much believes the same thing, there are so many denominations, many of whom want nothing to do with each other.

It was pretty clear that Sister Camille didn't totally agree with my concept of the Trinity. But she didn't tell me I was wrong. She always encouraged me to keep asking questions, to keep thinking about these things, to dig deeper and deeper. I did, but always with her. Two vastly different individuals forming an unlikely union. Connected to a divine energy. Committed to sharing it with others. A blessed trinity.

Perhaps feeling as if she hadn't adequately answered all my questions about other religions, Sister shared something she learned from the writings of Krister Stendahl, a Lutheran bishop from Stockholm. She called them his three rules for understanding another person's faith:

1. When you want to learn about a religion, ask its adherents, not its enemies.

2. Don't compare your best with their worst.

3. Leave room for "religious envy"—meaning leave room for something in another person's religion that you wish you had in your own religion.

I saw an opening. "Sister, what if we took the very best of Christianity from the West and combined that with the best from the East: Buddhism, Taoism, Hinduism and formed our own religion?"

"We already have," she quickly responded with a twinkle in her eye.

"We call it the Franciscans.

7

POLITICS IS NOT A RELIGION

I grew up in a hard-working family that ran a variety of small businesses. We weren't really that political, but if you pressed us hard enough, you would probably discover that we leaned slightly to the right of center. While we likely voted GOP most of the time, our real loyalty was to GSD: getting shit done. We all learned that through hard work and laws that protected the free markets, you could make a decent living, as well as provide jobs for others. I guess that makes me a Republican, but if you saw a picture on the wall of my office, you might think otherwise. In it, I'm posing with Jim Doyle, the 44th governor of Wisconsin and a Democrat. We traveled together to China to meet with the chairman of their equivalent to the chamber of commerce, and I asked Jim if we could get our picture taken with the chairman.

"Sure, as long as you don't share it with your Republican buddies back home," he laughed.

Naturally, I ignored his request and still take a lot of heat from those buddies who think I'm some sort of traitor now.

My political leaning towards the right just made sense to me. I was a proud free-market capitalist. Anti "big government." Didn't like the way the Democrats thought the only solution to a problem was to spend money. Yours and mine. And I've put my time and resources behind my convictions, having been involved in local and state politics throughout my career.

While most of my Republican views were inherited and served me well as a business owner, I really believed them. You've heard the term RINO (Republican in name only). I wasn't one of those. For me, being a Republican meant I was right, and those guys in the other party were wrong. I loved being right, maybe even more than I loved being a Republican. It also made things a lot easier because if you were a Democrat, I knew right away that you were part of the problem. The only way to solve the problem is to run your party out of office. End of discussion, literally. If a Democrat legislator in my state sponsored a bill, there was no need for me to read the bill or learn anything about it. I knew it was nothing more than liberal hogwash and urged my Republican allies in the State House of Representatives to vote it down.

Isn't it fun being right?

Being a good Republican from Wisconsin, I supported Senator Paul Ryan's campaign when he was on the ticket with presidential candidate, Mitt Romney in the 2012 election. In fact, it was Romney and Ryan's loss to Barak Obama that encouraged me to talk to Sister Camille about one of those topics we go out of our way to avoid, unless you're that uncle who shows up for Thanksgiving dinner and turns it into one big interfamily melee by showcasing his unpopular political views.

It wasn't just Obama's victory that got under my skin. A local reporter had been publishing some really critical pieces about Ryan and Romney, even after they lost the election. I had known this guy, who I'll call Dan, over the years and thought he was generally a fair-minded reporter—meaning he seemed like he might be a Republican—, so it felt to me like a betrayal. How could he possibly criticize "our" side who was right about so many things when he was supposedly an objective reporter. I got into a bit of a public spat with him, even confronting him at some big social event downtown, letting him and everyone else who was listening know what I thought of him. As far as I was concerned, I wasn't just defending Ryan and Romney, I was standing up for all Republicans. After all, there's a reason we're known as the *right* wing, not the wrong one.

I knew that Sister Camille had some Republican roots through her family, but as president of a university, she had to be able to work with—and seek financial support—from Republicans and Democrats alike. No one really knew where she stood politically, but I had a hunch that she was sympathetic to the Republicans and would understand why I was so upset over the election. Her father was a banker, so she was raised much like I was, learning the merits of free enterprise and limited government. As a college president, she networked with all the business leaders in the community. She was president of our predominately male downtown Rotary Club and first female president of the Chamber of Commerce. I was pretty certain she was just as concerned as I was that the country was now being run by a Democrat and that we would console each other even as we began scheming, like every other Republican, to make sure he was a one-term president.

The plan was to pick Sister up at her office and then drive to one of her favorite restaurants for lunch. I had discovered early on in our relationship that she loved a well-made gin martini, one olive.

I figured she would need a drink to talk politics, especially after our beloved party took such a whipping. Or maybe I was projecting, because after I finished my little rant about Obama and the Democrats and that turncoat reporter and all the other liberal media, she sat there for a moment, smiling. Smiling! This was serious business. The country had just elected a guy who was about to set a record for the number of new regulations imposed on businesses like mine. He had just accumulated the largest deficit of any president ever and was pro-choice, for God's sake! And she's smiling. Before she spoke, she reached over and gently touched my arm.

"Never forget, dearie, that politics and religion are like swimming pools— most of the noise comes from the shallow end."

I had to admit, that was pretty funny, and probably set me up for what followed.

"I understand your frustration. But I think it would help if you try to look at this election from both perspectives. I've learned that each person develops a political point of view based on their experiences throughout their life. Those who voted for President Obama are human beings who grew up in families and situations that helped shape their views, just as you and I did."

She explained that politics are really narcissistic; that all politics are local. There's no such thing as national politics. People are geared politically on how it impacts one person—me. Me and my beliefs. She went on to say that most priests and nuns in the Catholic church are Democrats, likely because they grew up either in poverty or at least not in privilege. Instead of dismissing them as the enemy, she counseled, I should try and understand why they believe the way they do.

"I try hard to remain non-partisan—remember Joe, I'm in higher education. I find Republican policies to generally be helpful but have also learned a lot from our Democratic friends. Along the way you will see that neither party is all good or all bad. Each has something of value to contribute, and we're all better off if we try to see things from each other's perspective."

Coming from her it made so much sense. In reality, those were truthful words I needed to hear, and it began a conversion of sorts, from being a guy who always has to be right to becoming more connected with people from all walks of life. Even as she spoke, my demeanor changed. When we entered that restaurant, I was angry, agitated, ready for some good revenge talk. Her voice, and her words had a calming effect on me. The anxiety I felt at the prospect of four years of Democratic rule literally evaporated. We might as well have been talking about a movie we both loved or the beloved birds that came to her feeder instead of politics.

Our conversation wasn't at all about politics, but about something she called "duality," or the tendency to see everything as black and white. You're a Catholic or a Protestant. A Packer fan or a Bears fan. A Republican or a Democrat. A capitalist or a socialist. She helped me see that most conflicts or disagreements are not as diametrically opposed as we make them. Instead of looking at something, such as party politics, as an either/or proposition, we should see it rather as both/and. In other words, both sides usually have something helpful or positive to offer, and we will miss that if we simply dismiss a particular point of view because we want to win or be right. You can be a Packer fan yet cheer for other NFL teams. You can be a Democrat yet understand the Republican viewpoint.

"Are we strong enough to hold together the tension of the paradox?" she asked, which was her very kind and gentle way of saying, "Oh dearie, don't be so afraid of what you might learn from the other side."

And that's how she lived. She resided in this place of calmness amidst the many conflicts that go with the territory of being a leader. She was fully aware of the dualities around her but always looked for the good that each side brought to the table. That ability requires enormous humility, the willingness to admit you might be wrong.

"Don't believe everything you think," she laughed. "Because not everything you think is true."

By the time we finished our lunch, my blood pressure was back to normal. Just listening to her had that effect on me, but more importantly, what she counseled began to change the way I looked at things. Over the next several days, I found myself engaging in conversations with colleagues that I knew were Democrats. Where in the past I would avoid engaging with them about politics, I now wanted to know more about why they believed the way they did. When they explained some of their views to me, I practiced a little technique that Sister taught me by responding, "Hmmm, I never really thought of it that way." Trust me, that worked a whole lot better than "How in the hell could anyone with half a brain believe that shit?" But it was more than a trick to avoid an argument. Thanks to Sister, I found myself genuinely interested in ideas that I personally had not embraced. That's not to say I changed my views, though I think I've mellowed drastically on some things. Instead, I began to appreciate the gift that comes with genuine dialogue as opposed to arguments.

Here's where it gets fun.

Remember Dan, that reporter who never missed an opportunity to slam my good Republican candidates, Mitt Romney and Paul Ryan? I was still holding a grudge over his reporting. If I saw him at an event, I would turn and walk away. I don't think I'm capable of detesting anyone, but I came pretty close with him. I just couldn't believe any intelligent person could criticize two fine, upstanding guys who I hoped would be leading our nation. But after talking with Sister Camille, I couldn't get her words out of my mind whenever I thought of Dan: "Look at it from his perspective." That's a bit hard to do if you turn your back on the guy every time you see him. Yet I couldn't ignore something else that Sister said: "When you meet face to face, easier to see eye to eye." I knew what I had to do, but it took a while before I summoned the courage to go see him at his office.

As we exchanged greetings, I could see that he looked at me warily, and why not? The last time we talked was at a very public event where I let him know what I thought of his reporting. He probably thought I dropped by to give him another dose, but to his credit he invited me to sit down.

"Dan, I'm here because I just don't feel right about the way I spoke to you about your coverage of Romney and Ryan."

I thought he was going to fall off his chair. We ended up talking for about an hour—had a great conversation as he explained why he felt his coverage was fair but understood he upset a lot of people. And you know what? I listened. I didn't totally agree with him but was able to see him and his reporting in a new light. Like a lot of journalists, he leaned to the left. Like a lot of businesspeople, I leaned to the right. I don't think I had ever asked someone with whom I disagreed to explain his or her views, but by listening to Dan, I got a better understanding of why he thought the way he did. Inexplicably, I also gained a new friend. That's right. A pretty conservative Republican and a liberal Democrat, once at odds with each other, now friends. When my third book, *After Further Review*, came out Dan published a feature article on it. Later, after he became editor a much larger newspaper, he published another feature on me. Then about a year later, Dan was considering a career change and came to me for some coaching. Once at odds with each other, now when we see each other, we hug.

As I write this, our nation is about as deeply divided as it's ever been in my lifetime. The Democrats are absolutely certain that they're right, and therefore they won't support any bill sponsored by a Republican. And the Republicans are absolutely certain that *they're* right and won't get behind anything supported by a Democrat. So sadly, nothing gets accomplished. Think of it, all of these intelligent people that we sent to Washington, and they can't do anything. Gone are the days when Speaker of the House, Tip O'Neill—a Democrat—and President Ronald Reagan—a Republican—would meet for drinks in one of their offices at the end of the day. Maybe that's why on a wall in my office I have a framed photograph of Reagan and O'Neill laughing together. Despite their differences, they had three things in common: a sense of humor, their Irish heritage, and the generous consumption of alcohol. They practiced what Sister Camille taught me to do. Listen to the other guy. Try to see things from his perspective. Don't always believe what you think.

But it's not just our politicians that need to pay attention to Sister Camille. We all do. My little joke earlier about that uncle who shows up and turns Thanksgiving dinner into a free-for-all? It's not really that funny because stuff like that actually happens. It's not that everyone sitting around the table for a family dinner agrees about everything. We don't, but we're afraid to talk about anything but the weather because we know it will end up in a big fight. What a shame, because whenever we avoid talking about the things that really matter to us, we miss opportunities to grow deeper in our relationships with family and friends.

I'm still a believer in free enterprise, but I'm no longer as rigid and close-minded as most Republicans. Rather, I would describe myself as a non-partisan who believes in free enterprise and no longer sees things in black and white. In fact, during our most recent election, I supported two Democrats. I saw one of them in a grocery store and told him how much I respected him and that I was going to send a check to his campaign. He lost the election, but when I saw him later on the tennis courts, he ran over and gave me a big hug. I looked around to make sure none of my Republican buddies saw that (just kidding).

"You're one of a very few from the other side who has ever contributed to my campaign," he told me. "Thank you."

I supported him because he's a terrific human being, and that has become more important to me than politics. I don't agree with some of his political views, but I had learned from Sister Camille to try and see things from his point of view. It helped me realize that he's as passionate about serving our nation as my Republican friends are, and if he runs again, I'll support him. And I sometimes wonder what would happen if each of us would deliberately seek out someone with whom we disagree politically, share a meal together, and really listen to them explain why they think the way they do. It's not that difficult, and it's a hell of a lot more fun than talking about the weather. Try it sometime, as Ellen DeGeneres so publicly did with George W. Bush at a Packers vs. Cowboys game.

By the way, the very day that I hugged a liberal Democrat and Ellen DeGeneres enjoyed a game with George W. Bush, I think the world began to see more clearly the hypocrisy we were engaging in as a nation. Might we be able to put our political and religious differences aside and enjoy friendships that cross all these manmade boundaries we've constructed?

One of the greatest examples of overcoming the tension in American politics is the letter George H. W. Bush (41) left on the presidential desk for Bill Clinton on his first day in office after a devastating defeat. The letter communicated that we are all one nation regardless of who is in the White House. Bill Clinton commented that he fell in love with George Bush from his handwritten, heartfelt letters. Want help getting past the political divisiveness? Read his letter.

THE WHITE HOUSE

WASHINGTON

Jan 20, 1993

Dear Bill,

When I walked into this
office just now I felt the same sense
of wonder and respect that I
felt four years ago. I know
you will feel that, too.

I wish you great happiness
here. I never felt the loneliness
some Presidents have described.

There will be very tough
times, made even more difficult by
criticism you may not think is fair.
I'm not a very good one to give
advice; but just don't let the
critics discourage you or push
you off course.

You will be our President
when you read this note. I wish
you well. I wish your family
well.

Your success now is our country's
success. I am rooting hard for you.
Good Luck —

George

8

I BELIEVE WE'VE MET BEFORE

One evening, I picked Sister up for dinner after returning from the wake of a friend. My mind was doing philosophical acrobatics contemplating all of the ideas surrounding death that I had been exposed to in life. As soon as she buckled herself in, I dove right into the hot topic of death. "Sister, what do you think happens when we die?"

In her typical reflective way, she paused and asked, "Why dearie, what do *you* think happens?"

"Well Sister, I have been trying to make sense of it since I was a kid."

When I was 15 years old, I read a book that made an enormous impact on me: *The Search for Bridey Murphy*. First published in 1956, it's the story of a woman named Virginia Tighe, a young housewife who lived in Denver. The book became an instant bestseller and later was turned into a popular movie by the same name. The author was a guy named Morey Bernstein who for a parlor trick, hypnotized Tighe by having her stare at a burning candle as he quietly told her that she was getting sleepy. Once she entered a trance-like state, he asked her to go back through space and time and tell him what she saw. What followed was nothing short of remarkable.

Immediately, this woman who had never been to Ireland began speaking in a rich Irish brogue. She recounted how she had been born in Cork, Ireland in 1798, the daughter of a lawyer. She went on to recite a rather complicated

Irish ancestry leading up to her own marriage to another Irish lawyer. I was transfixed as I read how she described in intimate detail the town of Cork, sharing the names and locations of dozens of shops and buildings throughout the city. According to the author, she even spoke a bit of Gaelic and then translated it for him. Before she finished, she claimed that she was the reincarnated Irish spirit of a woman named Bridey Murphy who had been dead for a couple of hundred years. It turned out that even though she had never been to Ireland, her descriptions matched exactly what Cork was like in the early nineteenth century.

Upon its release, the book generated a huge debate over its authenticity. If she was telling the truth, then just about everything we know about human existence is up for grabs. If this was a hoax, then the conventional wisdom about the human condition was correct: we are given one life and then it's gone.

I couldn't put the book down, and from that young age on, I never doubted her story. It made so much more sense to me than what I had been taught, which was that we basically get just one shot at life and then it's over. Reading about Virginia Tighe and Bridey Murphy sent me on a quest to learn about this thing called reincarnation, which at the time was brand new to me. I read everything I could get my hands on and came to realize that there were basically two schools of thought regarding human life and immortality. There was the view from the East that your soul needs to be developed and that for many, we have to come back several times until our souls become so fully developed that they could be united with this thing called God or divine energy. A great example of a fully-developed soul was St. Teresa of Calcutta who was connected with this divine energy at all times, even when she experienced times of doubt.

Then there's the Western view that most of us are accustomed to where you have one life and at the end you face either reward or punishment. In fairness, I researched this view as well, reading books about Christian doctrine, heaven and hell, purgatory, etc. The more I read, the less viable it seemed to me, especially in light of my research on reincarnation which led me to explore another phenomenon: near death experience or NDE. I read widely on this concept of people being given a glimpse into the other side, but the best book by far is

Dying to Be Me, by Anita Moorjani. After fighting cancer for four years, Moorjani's body began shutting down, and she was transported to another state where she was able to realize the inherent value of her soul. Remarkably, when she regained consciousness, her cancer was in remission and she was soon released from the hospital cancer free. One thing all those books on NDE had in common was the beauty that awaits all of us on the other side of our lives here on earth. As one NDE survivor put it, "If you ever see how beautiful it is after you die, none of us would ever cry at a funeral."

When I shared this with Sister Camille, she smiled slyly and said, "You're not going to cry at *my* funeral, are you?" In fact, I shared some of my thoughts about reincarnation with Sister, and it was clear that she didn't see life and death exactly the same way I did. But she never criticized or corrected me, rather she encouraged me to dig deep and keep an open mind, adding, "The truth is, dearie, we'll never know for sure until we die."

Part of my digging led me to a therapeutic technique called a "past life regression analysis." I learned that this is a legitimate form of therapy where a patient is hypnotized and then asked questions about the past. Now if you believed the Western view that we only have one life, you'd likely never consider submitting to this type of therapy. But I was growing more and more convinced not only with the Eastern view, but that I have somehow been here before. In fact, when I first met Sister Camille, I thought to myself, "She seems really familiar to me. How come I feel as if I already know her?" I also, for whatever reason, began to feel as if I had lived during World War II. I decided to seek out a professional who had experience in past life regression analysis and ultimately set up an appointment to meet with Susan Wisehart at her office in Chicago.

When I arrived, she took me into tastefully decorated room and invited me to lie down on a couch; she sat in a chair across from me. For about a half hour we just talked about the technique and what I could expect, and then she dimmed the lights a bit and told me just to relax and try not to think about anything in particular. Eventually, I fell into a deeply-relaxed state that some professionals refer to as the "alpha" state of the brain, which is basically where brain activity slows down. It was at this point that Susan instructed me to "walk off the bridge," then look down at my feet and tell her what I saw.

"I'm wearing army boots," I told her.

"Where are you?" she asked.

"I'm in a field," I replied, then I began to shake. My entire body. And it startled me.

"Susan, what's going on? Why am I shaking?"

"I don't know," she answered. "Tell me more."

Even though she recorded the entire hour-and-a-half session, to this day I remember everything I saw. It was as if I was floating above the earth, watching myself in this horrible war scene. As I tried to describe what I was seeing, I kept shaking all over, and then I recalled only two other times that my body had shook like that. In 1999, I went to see the movie, *Saving Private Ryan*, and as the troops landed on Omaha Beach, I began shaking so badly that I thought maybe I was afflicted with Parkinson's disease. The scenes were scary, that's for sure, but I had gone to scarier movies and never had this reaction. I honestly thought something was wrong with me physically, but the shaking stopped as soon as the movie was over.

Then in 2016 I visited Normandy with the U.S. Navy SEALs. I had worked with them as a consultant for a few years, and this was to be one of those unbelievable experiences of visiting hallowed ground with some of the toughest guys on the planet. I was really excited about it, but the moment we arrived, I began shaking again. What the hell, I thought. Is it the Parkinson's thing coming back? Or maybe I was having a stroke.

Susan interrupted my reverie with another assignment.

"Joe, let's take you back before this war scene. Where are you now—three, two, one, go."

"Oh my god! I'm in this beautiful field of butterflies."

"Really? Where is it?"

"I'm in St. Francis, Pennsylvania."

And then I went on to tell her that I was in this big meadow, that I was about six years old, and that I was with a little girl who was maybe four. It made no sense to me, but in a way, it seemed so familiar. So real.

Susan interrupted me again.

"Now let's move forward a few years, are you ready? Three, two, one go. What do you see?"

This time I was eighteen years old, and I was with that little girl again, only now she was about sixteen. I had just told her that I had enlisted in the army and would be leaving to go off to war.

"Oh, please come back and see me after the war is over," she pleaded.

I reassured her that I would, but I knew I would never return.

Susan interrupted again and asked me to move forward, and I soon found myself on the battlefield, and I began shaking again, uncontrollably, as I watched myself creeping forward on the beach with my platoon. We took a break hidden behind some rocks, and I used the time to take off my boots and socks to dump the sand out. Then we moved out, and in an instant, our platoon leader was shot and killed. I was now in command of our unit.

"Susan, I think we're on a suicide mission. I don't think we're going to get out of here alive."

Then I got really agitated and screamed at her, "What the hell is going on, Susan?"

I'll never forget her answer.

"Your soul is processing the trauma."

I continued describing what I saw, even telling her that I could smell the dead bodies around me. I had never in my life smelled a dead body, but that day it was all around me. The carnage was awful, worse than any scene from a movie. It was real. I was there. And then an explosion. Now I was above the battlefield rather than on it. I could see the explosions, hear the gunfire. But I was no longer part of it.

And I had stopped shaking.

It was as if I was floating, and instead of being filled with fear, I was overwhelmed with feelings of peace, joy, and contentment. The flashes of artillery fire slowly morphed into a bright white light, more brilliant than anything I had seen before. Susan asked me to describe what was going on, but for a few moments, all I could do was groan. It was the most beautiful feeling I had ever had in my life, and I didn't want to leave, but eventually, I returned, finding myself sitting up now on the couch, a little sheepish at what I just discovered. I was barefoot. Just as I had done on Omaha Beach, I had taken my shoes and socks off. Susan and I talked for a few minutes about what all of this meant and what I thought of it, and then I thanked her and left.

If this sounds a little out there to you, it wasn't to me. It was as real as anything I've experienced in my life, one of the most transforming events that has ever happened to me. As I drove home I recalled something that Dr. Wayne Dyer said: "If you can connect with the life force, you'll never die because when your present body ceases to live, you go back into that force and wherever life is, you'll be there." Those words made sense when I first read them; they became crystal clear to me after I was given a glimpse into what may have been a previous life of mine. I felt more connected than ever to life itself, becoming even more convinced that life is not a single journey that ends in death but a series of excursions that are developing are souls into an eternal connection with the divine.

My experience with Susan Wisehart also shed some light on how I got my name. When I was two years old, my parents gave me a G.I. Joe uniform. At the time, he was all the rage with kids like me, and I practically slept in it. Wore it all the time. My given name was Gary, but after getting that little uniform, I told anyone who would listen, "My name's not Gawy. It's G.I. Joe." I must have worn them all down, including my parents and siblings because from then on, I've been Joe. Coincidence? Foreshadowing? Who knows?

Of course, I couldn't wait to share my past life regression analysis with Sister Camille, and that opportunity came about two weeks later when I met her at Clare Hall and walked with her over to the little bench beneath a grove of trees. I gestured for her to sit down, but she asked if we could take a walk. It was a gorgeous Indian summer afternoon, so we continued down the sidewalk as I began to describe what had happened. I told her everything. About the shaking. About shedding my shoes and socks. About the little girl in the field of butterflies. About going off to war and never returning. She listened intently, maybe even more than usual.

After I finished, she motioned to another bench and we sat down as the sun warmed us in the gentle breeze. She said nothing for almost a full minute, looking off into the distance as if she was trying to remember something. For a moment, I thought that maybe she was trying to come up with a kind and polite way to tell me I'd lost my marbles. And then she spoke.

"Oh dearie, I find that so fascinating, for a lot of reasons. It sounds to me that you might think you had a previous life as a soldier. If that's true, and I'm not sure how we determine if it is or not, that certainly adds a new dimension to what I believe about life and death."

I could see that she took my experience seriously and rather than dispute it, she entertained the possibility that we not only live forever, as her church taught, but that our eternal lives might be manifest in ways consistent with the Eastern concept of reincarnation. In other words, she left the door open. I loved that about her. I get so turned off by the certainty of organized religion and how all religious groups have to be right. She never said, "I believe in reincarnation," but at the same time, she didn't brush off the idea the way so many religious people do.

We talked for a while about death and dyin but not in a morbid way. She explained that while she didn't fear death, she wasn't in a hurry to see what it was like. And we both agreed that the only ones who know for sure what happens when you die, are those who have died. But then she added something that only adds to the mystery of this subject.

"You know, dearie," she began. "Many years ago, when I was a young girl, I had a boyfriend who joined the Army. He went off to war and never came back."

Before I could respond, she continued.

"You don't suppose. . . ."

9

NAUGHTY BUT NICE

When friends who knew me well learned that I had developed a close relationship with a nun, the response was always the same.

"You? And a nun? Get outta here!"

Or something like that. They knew me. They knew some nuns. And the image of the two of us together just didn't compute. Although I've gone to church all my life, I have at times been critical of the Church's teachings. I'm not real proud of this, but I, um, occasionally use a little profanity. Who am I kidding? I swear a lot more than I like to admit, and anyone who's attended Catholic school knows what happens when you swear around a nun. I can still feel that ruler on my knuckles. To anyone who knows anything about nuns and about me, the idea that I would change my schedule just to spend time with an elderly nun just didn't make sense. But then, they didn't know Sister Camille.

While Sister was perhaps the most deeply spiritual person I've ever known, she had a bit of a naughty side to her, though I may need to qualify that. By naughty, I don't mean to imply that she did anything that violated her vows to the Church or that she harbored some sort of secret vice. Her "naughtiness" was more along the lines of surprising you with her humanity. We have this image of priests and nuns as residing on some lofty pedestal where all they do is pray the Rosary or meditate on God, which of course they do, minus the pedestal.

When Sister prayed the prayer of St. Francis, it was as if God himself was present. In fact, it is such a sacred moment that I asked her if I could capture it on the video function of my cell phone. I watch and listen to it every morning when I shave. When I share about her naughty side, I do not want give the impression that she was anything but the modern-day saint I believe she was.

But as I learned from Sister, saints like to have fun.

I've already mentioned her love for the traditional gin martini, straight up with an olive. And on occasion, followed by another one. It likely caught a few people by surprise to see this deeply spiritual nun sipping on her favorite drink at a public event, but she didn't care. She enjoyed it, never tried to hide it, and I think took a little guilty pleasure in knowing that she was crushing the stereotype people have about nuns. A favorite of the local media, one time a reporter somehow noticed that she had just ordered a second martini and asked her why.

"Because I *like* them!" she laughed.

Sister loved a good joke and could deliver a punch line with perfect timing. For example, she adored Barbara Bush, and in a few pages, I'll share how I was able to help her reconnect with the President and First Lady. But on this particular occasion, I joined Sister at her residence in Clare Hall to watch Mrs. Bush's funeral. The local NBC affiliate knew of Sister's relationship with Mrs. Bush and showed up to interview her, then film her watching the funeral. Everyone was appropriately solemn and respectful as we watched the beautiful ceremony broadcast from St. Martin's Episcopal Church in Houston. I had brought some photographs and other memorabilia that I had from the Bushes, and after the funeral I passed them around to the reporter and photographer from NBC. Jokingly, the photographer pointed to President Bush and asked Sister, "Who's that guy?" Without missing a beat, she deadpanned, "I'm not sure, but I think it might be Mrs. Bush's husband."

Sister Camille being interviewed by NBC, showing her humor by saying the
man in the photo is Barbara Bush's husband.

Sister loved to laugh, even if the joke was on her. On one of my many visits
to Clare Hall, we had just gone to Mass and gathered in the dining room for
the evening meal. For whatever reason, Sister was in what I would call a silly
mood. I remember once talking with her about humor and she said that if
nothing else, humor is good for our physical, spiritual, and emotional well-be-
ing, and on this evening, she clearly was enjoying herself. As I always did, I had
stopped and bought a case of wine for the sisters. It was sort of our little thing.
I would go around with a bottle and each nun would hold up her glass and
say, "Just a wee bit, Joe," then I'd deliver what is known as a generous pour,
which probably explains why they were such an approving audience that night
to Sister's mischief, which included French fries.

I don't know if you've ever seen the movie, *The Lady and the Tramp*, but there's a scene where the two dogs, from opposite sides of the tracks, nuzzle over a plate of spaghetti and end up slurping the same noodle until they meet at the middle and "accidentally" kiss. As sister ate her dinner, whenever she picked up a French fry, she would hold it between her lips and turn toward me with that sly grin I had come to know. We would all laugh, and then she would finish eating the French fry. But she kept doing it, so after about the fifth time I looked at her in mock consternation and scolded, "If you do that one more time, Sister, I'm going to come over there and eat that French fry right out of your mouth!"

Of course, you know what happened, and the nuns almost fell off their chairs they were laughing so hard. Unfortunately, one of the sisters snapped a picture of it as evidence. She sent it to me and every time I look at it, I call it my Lady and the Tramp picture, and we all know I'm the tramp.

The Lady and the Tramp We all know who the tramp is here!

With Sister, naughty sometimes meant rebellious, as I learned when she fell and broke her hip. As soon as I heard she was in the hospital, I paid her a visit to make sure everything was okay. She was obviously in a lot of pain, and I wasn't sure if it was her hip or the fact that she was confined to her hospital room. The next day I got a call from her.

"Come down and get me out of her now!" she demanded in a voice that told me she meant business.

"Why Sister, what's wrong?"

"I need to go home. Now! I miss my bed. I miss the sisters. I told my doctor I don't want to be here, but he won't listen to me. Come get me and take me home."

I knew she must be serious because in all the years I had known here, I'd never known her to be demanding. Just the opposite. She always put other people's needs before her own, but she made it very clear that I had better get my you-know-what to the hospital and figure out a way to break her out of there.

I drove to the hospital and first sought out her doctor, and he told me in no uncertain terms that Sister needed to stay in the hospital. In fact, he suggested I try to talk her out of leaving. I then took the elevator to her floor, and as I walked into her room, she practically shouted at me: "Don't you dare try to talk me out of leaving. Get me out of here!"

I found the doctor again and told him it was no use. She was going home to-day and needed her discharge papers. He sighed, reminding me that a woman her age with a broken hip could face serious complications if she didn't remain in the hospital, then reluctantly he handed me the authorization that would allow me to take her home. By the time I got back to her room, she was already in a wheelchair. "Let's go, dearie!"

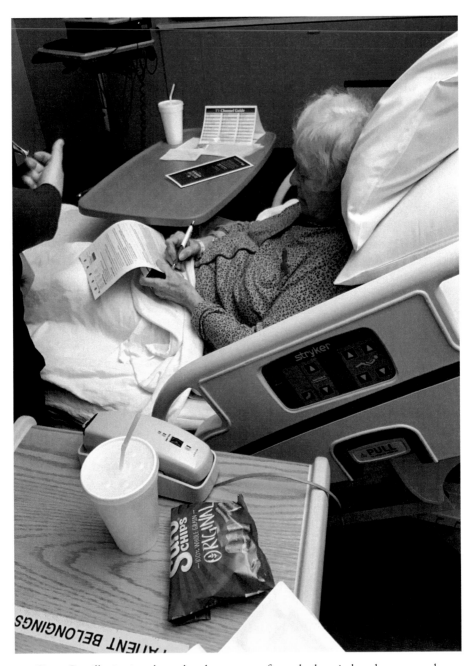

Sister Camille signing the early release papers from the hospital as she expressed,
"It was like escaping from a prison."

I followed her as an attendant pushed her down the hall, into the elevator, and over to the entrance, then I sprinted to the parking garage to get my car. When I pulled up to the entrance, it suddenly dawned on me. How am I going to get her from the wheelchair into the passenger seat of my car? Her hip was broken, for crying out loud. She couldn't put any weight on it, meaning she couldn't walk from the chair to the car. Praying that I wasn't violating any hospital or church protocol, I lifted her up from the chair and carried her the three steps to my car, gingerly depositing her in the seat. I then ran over to the driver's side, hopped in, and hit the gas before looking over to make sure she was alright, only to see her smiling widely with her right hand held up high awaiting my response for a high-five.

"Oh dearie," she laughed. "That was so much fun. Now I know what it must be like for the bad guys to break out of prison."

Sister seemed to really enjoy bending the hospital's rules, so a few years later I decided to take that rebellious concept one step further. She absolutely loved going out to eat, and I took her out often to Milwaukee's best restaurants. When she turned ninety, we celebrated her birthday at her favorite restaurant, Carnevor. As we waited to be seated, I quietly informed the maître d' that it was my "girlfriend's" 90th birthday. They, of course, all knew us, since we ate there so often, so the guy winked and then seated us. After a wonderful meal accompanied as always by lively conversation, a parade of servers and the head chef arrived at our table carrying a birthday cake, complete with candles. Sister was thrilled, so much so that a week later, when I took her out for dinner, I surreptitiously repeated the birthday story to the maître d', and once again, dessert was served up with a surprise birthday cake.

"Oh dearie, you mustn't lie to these good people. It's not really my birthday."

"Not so loud Sister. They might hear you. Besides, when you're ninety, every day's your birthday."

After the age of 90, every day is your birthday.

I had to be careful for the rest of the year because I didn't want to get caught telling the same story twice to a maître d'. It really didn't matter because I suspect they knew all along of my little ruse. What was even better is that because Sister was so well known in the community, every time the servers brought out a birthday cake, nearly everyone in the restaurant would stand and sing the birthday song to her, holler out birthday greetings, even offer to buy her a drink. By about the fourth birthday celebration, Sister Camille appeared to have grown not only accustomed to but quite fond of our deception.

Because of my work, I was sort of forced to make all the rounds when it came to social events in Milwaukee. While these fundraisers and community soirees provided opportunities to let your hair down a bit, they always felt like work to me. But hanging out with Sister at a nice restaurant was one of my life's great pleasures. She was just so much fun. Someone once asked me if I cleaned up my act around her. The answer is pretty much no. I never felt I had to be anyone but myself when I was with her, but one time, I thought maybe I had pushed the limits of her tolerance for naughtiness.

We were on another of our dinner dates, and to get things started Sister Camille ordered two martinis. Now I don't drink martinis, and when those two rather large glasses of alcohol arrived, all I could think was if I drink that, I'll probably do or say something I'll later regret. We clinked our glasses in a little toast, then I took the tiniest of sips. Sister, meanwhile, finished hers rather quickly. She must have been really thirsty or something because that was the first time I saw her do that. When she saw that I wasn't finishing my drink she asked, "Oh dearie, is there something wrong with your drink?"

"Oh, it's fine Sister, but I think that's about all I can handle."

I barely got the words out of my mouth when she reached over, daintily picked up my glass, and drank it! I couldn't believe it. I was already feeling tipsy over the little that I drank. How is this woman even conscious? There we were, with two empty glasses in front of us, and for whatever reason—maybe it was the alcohol talking—I asked her a question.

"Sister, do you know how a martini and a woman's breasts are alike?"

"Her eyes literally danced as she answered, "Why no, dearie. Tell me."

"One is never enough and three are too many."

She laughed so hard I thought she'd pass out.

Over the years, I've developed some personal rituals that help center me spiritually. Largely due to my relationship with Sister Camille, but also through my friendship with Cardinal Timothy Dolan, I added another, and that is a question we ask ourselves at the end of the day: "What is one thing I did today to create a belly laugh?" Really spiritual, huh? Actually, I believe it is. Sister and I talked a lot about the value of humor. She saw it as a great gift that comes directly from God that has many practical benefits. People in stressful jobs—and you can add college president to that list—generally fare better if they have developed a sense of humor. There's also a lot of research on how humor actually has a healing effect by releasing dopamine and serotonin. With Sister, humor was an integral part of being human, reminding us not to take ourselves too seriously but to enjoy the lighter moments that surround us if only we take the time to look for them.

As I prepared for a trip to visit Assisi, the home of Sister Camille's beloved St. Francis, I had a brainstorm. I drove over to Clare Hall and got Sister and the nuns together and told them about my upcoming trip. Then I told them I'd like to take a group photo of them and hang it on the wall of the church where he was buried.

The Sisters of St. Francis, St. Francis, WI.

"Oh dearie, they'll never let you do that." Sister cautioned.

I convinced them to at least let me take the picture, then left to the sounds of the sisters bidding me farewell and asking me to say hello to St. Francis for them. It was really a fun send off for my pilgrimage to the home of a saint I had come to love almost as much as Sister did.

When I got to the church, I was greeted by a young monk whose job was to show visitors around and plead for a couple of euros to help maintain the church. I soon discovered that Sister Camille was right. When I pulled out the picture and asked if I could place it on the wall, the little monk frowned.

"Oh, I'm afraid we can't do that," he cautioned.

I reached for my wallet, pulled out a hundred euro note, and asked him if he was absolutely certain we couldn't find a way to hang the picture on the wall. His demeanor changed ever so slightly.

"I think we might be able to find a place for it."

Photo of the Sisters of St. Francis in St. Francesco Basilica in Assisi, Italy.

We were sitting at a table in the basement near the actual grave of the beloved saint, and given the monk's, um, appreciation for euros, I decided to go for it. I walked over to the grave and placed the photo directly in it.

Placing the photo of the Sisters in the tomb of St Francis.

"How about here?" I asked.

"That won't be possible," he said, shaking his head.

I reached into my wallet for another hundred euro note and handed it to him.

"I believe it would look very nice there," he nodded as we both admired my handiwork.

I took a picture of it, and when I got back to the States, I dropped by Clare Hall and as the nuns gathered around me, I showed them their picture in the very grave of St. Francis and told them they'd be sleeping with St. Francis forever (though I'm pretty certain the monk removed the picture soon after I left).

"Oh dearie," Sister exclaimed. "How on earth did you get them to let you put our picture in his grave?"

"As you know, Sister, the Lord works in mysterious ways."

Her wink told me that she knew damn well I had bribed a monk. And that I was forgiven.

10

WHAT'S A CATHOLIC WITHOUT A LITTLE SHAME AND GUILT?

The short answer? Not a Catholic.

Catholics in particular, but Christians of all stripes, have mastered the fine art of shame and guilt. You skipped church last Sunday? Shame on you! You were too busy to read the Bible this morning? Shame on you! You're not going on the men's retreat? Shame on you! You're not sending your kids to our church's private school? Shame on you!

I used to joke that Catholics don't feel right unless they wake up feeling guilty for the first two hours of the day. Except it's not that funny. One of the reasons I've been uncomfortable with the Christian doctrine of original sin is that it tries to make me feel responsible for the death of Jesus. I just don't buy it. I'm supposed to feel guilty about something that happened 2,000 years ago? As I mentioned previously, it's like when I was eight-years old, getting ready for First Communion and Sister Almadeo was trying to explain that because of my sin, Jesus had to die.

I don't mean to be disrespectful, but it just doesn't make sense to try and guilt me into believing something. But that's basically what religions do to get others to join their tribe. When you stop and think about it, why would I want to be a part of your group if I have to first be ashamed of myself?

To be fair, however, this isn't just a church thing. Whether you're religious or not, shame and guilt lurk in the corners of your mind. Literally. It's just how the mind works. Your neighbor pulls into the driveway with a brand-new Mercedes, and all of the sudden your Lexus feels like a rust bucket off the bargain lot. Or you're feeling pretty good about taking your family to Vail to ski over the holiday break until you learn that your golfing buddy is headed to the Swiss Alps with his family. (All problems of the prosperous, by the way.) It's in our nature to focus on where we don't think we measure up, rather than to be content with our lives.

For example, every year between Thanksgiving and New Year's Day, I take a big look in the rear-view mirror. I call it my "Year in Review." I try to list all the positives I experienced over the past year, as well as the negatives. I usually end up with anywhere from 150-180 positives, and a much smaller list of maybe ten to 15 negatives. Guess what I focus on? Dammit, I should have closed that deal. What was I thinking when I bought that timeshare? Oh my God, that was the worst hire I've ever made. So many great things happened the previous year, but all I can do is agonize over the few things that went wrong.

That's what shame and guilt will do to you.

Social media doesn't help. As far as I'm concerned, Facebook should change its name to Fakebook because that's what's really going on there. I'm guilty of it too. You're sitting home eating leftovers, and you check your phone only to see me being served filet mignon at Carnevor with the president of Cardinal Stritch University. I may not be deliberately trying to make you feel guilty, but it doesn't matter. Your brain tells you what a sorry little life you have compared to mine. Then I check my phone and see that my best friend's kid got accepted to Harvard. You think my first reaction is "Gee, I'm so happy for him?" Not exactly. All I'm thinking is "Where did I go wrong?" Shame on me for not paying for a tutor. Shame on me for not helping him with advanced trigonometry (which would have been a disaster). Shame on me. Shame on me. Shame on me. Yet that's how many of us live.

Sister Camille and I talked about this a lot, usually with me confessing to her that I had really screwed something up and felt horrible about it.

"Oh dearie, all that shame and guilt you're carrying around. Those are two useless emotions. What have you ever gained from feeling ashamed or guilty? For a lot of people, it's an endless cycle that constantly makes us feel pretty lousy about ourselves, about our lives. Joe, what really creates shame and guilt is trying to live up to three fundamental lies:

1. I am what I have.

2. I am what I do.

3. I am what other people think of me.

I'm pretty sure you've run into those lies, maybe even believed them. You fill your garage with grown-up toys because what you own defines you. To be the best, you have to buy the best car, the best boat, the best set of golf clubs. Or you may be perfectly content doing a great job as a mid-level manager, but you go for the promotion, not because you want the job, but because of what it will say about you. And both of those lies are driven by the foundational one: your value and success as a human being is determined by others. By believing those lies, we set ourselves up for the kind of shame and guilt that prevents us from being our truest selves."

In fact, Sister explained that what should really make us feel shame is when we are not aligned with our truest self. All this trying to be what we're not is what ought to bother us, to the point we get back to being genuine, free from constantly seeking validation from others. That hit a little close to home, because in a way, I've felt some guilt over the career I chose. I probably should have become a behavioral psychologist, a basketball coach, even a Navy SEAL. Those things were much closer to who I was than going into business. But my mind said, "I've gotta go into the business world. I need to make a lot of money." Fortunately, I must have inherited some of my dad's business skills, and I did alright. So maybe there was a little business in my truest self. And the good news is that finally, after all those years in business, I'm doing more of the things that I love. But my point is that true guilt should come from not being a genuine, authentic person. Being human means we will make mistakes, but instead of wallowing in guilt over them, we need to pick ourselves up, seek forgiveness if necessary, and get back to being who we were created to be, warts and all.

"Most people really try to do their best every day," Sister counseled. "That's all we can expect of ourselves, and if you mess up today, you always have tomorrow. Shame only makes things worse. The best definition of success is living your truest self every day."

It brought to mind a friend of mine whose son was graduating from high school. He and his wife invited friends and relatives to an open house in their son's honor, and a former neighbor from a neighboring state drove nearly 200 miles to attend the open house. My friend was thrilled to see the former neighbor, and the two of them grabbed some time together away from the other guests. Feeling a little vulnerable, he confided to the former neighbor, "Jim, this has been a rough year between my son and me, and I feel as if I've made every mistake a parent can make. I sure wish I could go back and undo some of the things I've said and done."

As my friend recounted, Jim leaned over and gave my friend a big hug and a huge dose of wisdom.

"Did you ever wake up in the morning and say to yourself, 'I'm going to do my best to screw up my son's life today?'"

Before my friend could answer, Jim continued.

"Of course, you didn't. Every decision you made regarding your son was the best you knew to do with the information you had at the time. Quit beating yourself up for trying you best."

A few years ago, I went with my brother, Mike, to a little hermitage in Mexico where we spent some time with one of my favorite authors, Father Richard Rohr. To this day I'm not sure what was behind his question, but Mike asked Fr. Rohr what he thought of shame and guilt. This deeply spiritual, modern-day mystic spoke eloquently.

"Awwwwww, it's just a bunch of crap."

We had a good laugh, but then Fr. Rohr continued.

"It's all about the ego, trying to prove you're right. Don't waste much time with shame. We all want to be perfect, or at least make others think we're perfect. But of course, we're not." In his book, *Falling Upward,* he talks about how in the first half of our lives, we build the ego while in the second half, our job is to tame it by serving others.

Most religions play right into this desire to be right. They produce what I call "box-checkers." You've got all these rules, and if you can just check them all off, you'll show everyone how good you are.

- Go to church. Check!

- Don't eat for one hour before communion. Check!

- No meat on Fridays. Check!

- Eat only kosher foods. Check!

- Pray five times a day. Check!

- Don't drink caffeinated beverages. Check!

- Wear special underwear when you enter the temple. Check!

Because no one can consistently follow all the rules of their religion, they're constantly struggling with shame and guilt. They're so worried about checking all the right boxes that they miss out on the joy and peace that religion is supposed to deliver. What a crazy way to live, but we all do it from time to time.

Bestselling author and researcher Brené Brown calls shame "the swampland of the soul." It's what keeps us from being all that we were created to be. Most of the great innovators and leaders in history were people who weren't afraid to fail, who refused to dare to do something others thought was impossible. As Brown puts it, in one of her recent talks, "Shame is the little gremlin that whispers in your ear, 'You're not good enough.'"

What is it that you wish you could do, or be, but you're afraid to give it a try because you might fail?

I asked Sister, "How do we minimize the harm shame can do?"

She responded, "I've learned that there are things we can do to minimize guilt and shame and live more closely aligned with our truest selves."

- First, become aware of it;

- Recognize that you can't eliminate it overnight;

- Focus more on what you've done right rather than on the mistakes you've made;

- Remind yourself that you are human, not a superpower; and

- Counter your shame with prayer, reflection, and meditation.

With shame so ever-present in religion, I asked Sister where it comes from, if it was something that came from God.

"Oh dearie, God is a loving God. He doesn't shame anybody. All he wants of you is to know you are loved and to help you love others more and become the best version of yourself."

I wanted to ask her if that's the case, why is there so much shame and guilt in the Church. If God reaches out to us with love, why don't his followers do the same? I think it has something to do with sin.

Sin . . . hmmm. Sounds like time for another meeting with Sister.

11

BLESS ME SISTER, FOR I HAVE SINNED - THE CONCEPT OF SIN

I may have given you the impression that Sister Camille and I agreed on everything. If I have, I need to be really clear. Not only did Sister occasionally disagree with me, she wasn't one to avoid confrontation, especially when we discussed some of the core teachings of her faith. She didn't back down, and one of those areas where we didn't see eye-to-eye was sin. As I mentioned in the previous chapter, I just don't believe in the Christian doctrine of original sin. That one man's sin (Adam) has stained all of us. And because of Adam's sin, Jesus had to die, making his death all my fault. I understand that this is a foundational doctrine for orthodox Christianity, but to me it doesn't make any sense, and I confessed this to sister in one of our times together, and her response is reason number 731 why I loved her so.

"Oh dearie, please help me understand why this is so hard for you to believe."

Let that sink in a little. I had just openly challenged one of the most basic truths of her faith. She was a nun, a prominent leader in the Catholic church, and I was this smartass business guy, who should have known better after twenty years attending Catholic schools. But instead of chastising me for denying such an important facet of her faith, she was genuinely curious and offered me the opportunity to explain myself. I was all geared up for a big argument, but now I actually had to engage in a conversation with someone who seemed to want to learn from me. Imagine having coffee with a few of your Democrat buddies, and you say something like, "You know, I really like some of the things that the current president is doing." How do you think they would respond?

Although Sister and I agreed on a lot of things, I think I learned more from her in our disagreements. I especially learned from her *how* to disagree in a way that has made me a better person. For a lot of my adult life, I was a fairly straightforward and direct guy. If you did something that I didn't like or thought was wrong, I'd tell you straight: "That's the stupidest thing I've ever heard." Of course, that only makes you dig your heels in deeper, and before you know it, we've got a pretty good argument going. What's really going on is that we both have to be right. I recall with more than a little regret doing something like that with one of my brothers. I'm not talking sibling rivalry when we were kids, but as a grown up that should know better. I don't even remember what the issue was; I just remember letting him have it and feeling awful later. Sister modeled a much better way to handle conflict. Whenever we disagreed, Sister never backed down yet never came right out and told me I was wrong. Trust me, I've had other religious people tell me pretty forcefully that I was wrong, especially younger priests fresh out of seminary who have all the answers. But Sister was refreshingly different when it came to our disagreements, and I asked her about that once.

"In life we have something called a paradox," she began. "A paradox occurs when two conflicting views comes at you at the same time. Because of our insecurities, we create an either-or dichotomy. I'm right, so you must be wrong. The challenge for us when it comes to paradox is to turn it into a both-and equation. Maybe we're both right. Or both wrong. Simply fighting over things—even really important things—never lets us learn from each other."

Those words she spoke several years ago appear even more relevant and helpful today, considering the way our culture is so divided. You're either a Republican or a Democrat. A Christian or a Jew. A saint or a sinner. Have we really gained anything by partitioning ourselves off into these little kingdoms of absolute truth? Are we really so arrogant as to believe there's nothing we can learn from that person whose views appear to oppose our own? When Sister refused to correct my "faulty" theology of sin, she literally disarmed me, allowing us to enjoy a civil discussion where both of us learned something. As I further explained my thoughts on original sin, she used a couple of other key phrases that challenged my thinking without declaring me wrong: "I'd like to invite you to consider. . . ." And perhaps my favorite: "In the spirit of continuous improvement. . . ." How can you argue against that?

Sister and I talked a lot about sin. It wasn't just original sin that bothered me, but the very definition of sin I'd been taught all my life. I mean, there's the Seven Deadly Sins. Breaking any of the Ten Commandments. There are mortal sins. And venial sins. Sin always seemed to me to be a long list of things you weren't supposed to do. But we did them all the time because we couldn't help it. Because of—you guessed it—original sin. It seemed like someone deliberately stacked the deck against us.

Then there were a whole bunch of other sins that other religions have added to the list over the years. The Amish can't drive cars or flip a switch to turn on the lights. There's a denomination that believes it's a sin to use instrumental worship in church. Another denomination teaches that it's a sin for women to braid their hair or wear slacks. I know a guy who grew up in a church where it was a sin to play cards, drink, or bet on the ponies. I think it was called the Church of No Fun. And of course, Baptists can't dance, but I don't know for sure if that's because it's a sin or because they're all white people.

Are you beginning to understand why I've spent most of my life trying to understand what sin is?

When I shared these thoughts with Sister, she at first defended her Church's teaching about sin.

"You certainly would agree that there are some really awful things—even evil things—that we should try not to do," she cautioned.

Of course, I had to agree with her. Many of the "sins" recognized by organized religion come from natural law, determining good from evil by observing nature. But is that really sin? The whole idea of natural law didn't originate with any religion, but with the Greek Stoic philosophers who lived about 300 years before Jesus. Indeed, our justice system, even the Constitution, derive from natural law. Breaking a law is a bad thing and will get you punished, but is that what sin is all about? I didn't think so, and as I pushed back a little on this with Sister, what she said not only surprised me, but basically reframed my whole thinking on sin.

"Maybe a better definition of sin would be separation. Separation from ourselves. From others. And maybe most important, separation from God or what you might prefer calling a power greater than ourselves."

She then went on to explain that the overarching message of the Bible is God calling us *to* him. To join him. To connect with him. It was like a light bulb went on in my soul. She was basically saying that sin is going it alone. To separate us from others and from God. All those lists of things we shouldn't do might help us avoid a lot of stuff that isn't good for us, but those are essentially the same things as a country club posting rules for its members to follow. Sin is really much more serious, more damaging. It's allowing yourself to be completely isolated, which isn't the same as solitude. Going off by yourself for a period of time is a healthy way to center yourself, to remain connected. Isolation deliberately breaks your connection to the divine, leaving you alone and alienated.

Sister's use of the Bible to explain this to me reminded me that I read the Bible because of what the letters in it stand for: Basic Instruction Before Leaving Earth.

Sister's explanation of sin made so much sense to me, and as I studied Father Richard Rohr's writings, he seemed to agree with her. "The great illusion that we must all overcome is that of separateness. Religion's primary task is to communicate *union*, to reconnect people to their original identity "hidden with Christ in God." (from *The Cosmic Christ,* by Richard Rohr)

And in another one of his meditations he wrote,

"Throughout much of the Bible "sin" is *perceived* as an objective state and "sinners" as a class of people. God's clear and specific job description is to undo separation: "My dear people, we are already the children of God; it is only what is in the future that has not yet been revealed, and then all we know is that we shall be like God" (1 John 3:2). Jesus is *The Great Reconnector*—by modeling his own objective connection with God and telling us to do the same."

The whole sin thing for me had been that "worthiness game where no one really wins." You were taught to just keep checking the boxes, hoping that someday you'll be good enough, which of course you never were because they either added new boxes, or you slipped up on the ones you had already checked. It seemed that the primary aim of the church was to tell me I was a sinner. It was so refreshing to hear these two wise servants of the church remind me that I am already a child of God. But as we, on several occasions, continued talking about sin, I learned that they weren't the only ones in the church who thought this way. We dove pretty deeply into the writings and teachings of some of the church's great saints: St. Francis of Assisi, St. Teresa of Ávila, St. John of the Cross, St. Ignatius of Loyola, and St. Teresa of Calcutta. Although they said it differently, if I had to sum up how they defined sin, it would be separateness.

Ironically, even some of the teaching about sin in the more fundamentalist Christian denominations echoes this theme of separateness. Baptist preachers and the like often talk about sinners as being lost. Lost imagery abounds in their sermons and songs, including a favorite that includes the line, "I once was lost but now am found." Have you ever been lost? Alone in the woods, not by choice but because you got turned around and you have no idea where you are? That's a perfect illustration of my new understanding of sin. You're cut off. Isolated. Alone.

A friend of mine shared the story of when he was a teenager and his dad took him on his first deer hunt. They drove a hundred or so miles to a remote spot in a national forest, bounced down a two-track road, then parked in a clearing. The plan was for his dad to stay on the two-track while he would trek into the woods, covering a long arc that would eventually bring him back to the road. He walked for what he estimated to be about a mile, curved around in the direction he was certain would bring him back to the spot but after walking for about three hours, the road was nowhere in sight. Almost in a panic, he realized he was lost. He tried to backtrack, but every hill and valley looked the same. Unwisely, he began running, only to become exhausted and even more frightened as it was beginning to get dark. He began calling out to his dad, pausing to listen for his voice. He tried walking in one direction for a few minutes, then another, then still another, calling out to his dad every few minutes. He knew his dad was out there somewhere. He just couldn't find him. Just when he was about to build a shelter to spend the night in the woods, he heard his dad calling out to him. He ran toward the voice and within minutes he was walking alongside his dad back to their car. After he shared that story, he told me being lost was one of the worst feelings he'd ever experienced, while being reunited with his dad was one of the best.

We all yearn to be connected to the divine energy that some refer to as the Heavenly Father.

Sin. Isolation. Separateness. It's a horrible place to be, yet we see it all around us. According to a news service for medical doctors, forty-seven percent of American adults are afflicted with loneliness. And it's not getting any better. Generation Z—those born after 1995—are considered to be the loneliest generation. I don't know this for sure, but I'd be willing to bet a lot of those lonely people are box checkers. Trying their hardest to be good, yet still afflicted with sin.

Here's the *real* good news: there's a way out of their sin, and it's a lot easier than they think.

12

I AM THE VINE: THE ART OF CONNECTION

A guy calls a party store and places an order:

"I'd like two fifths of bourbon. Three fifths of vodka. A case of beer. Four bottles of wine. And a fifth of gin."

"Golly," to clerk responded. Sounds like you're having a big party."

"Nope. I'm just trying to get up enough nerve to go to confession."

Not only do we have the wrong idea about sin, we go to a lot of crazy lengths to get rid of it. Of course, the Catholic sacrament of confession is probably the most well-known. This is where you go into a little chamber where a priest sits behind a screen and you tell him all the bad things you've done. He then forgives your sins and recommends "penance," something you have to do to make amends for those sins. That's probably oversimplifying a sacred ritual that many find helpful. The late Lee Iacocca, CEO and Chairman of Chrysler, regularly went to confession, and when a reporter once asked him why he did that, he answered "Confession to me is the examination of the conscience." Put that way, I'm a big fan of confession; something that I try to do every day with what I call my Seven Daily Questions."

But the so-called sin problem leads people to do a lot of strange things. Have you ever heard the phrase, "Don't beat yourself up?" Usually offered when someone makes a big mistake. Believe it or not, some people actually do that to get rid of their sins. Congregationalist writer, Sara Osborn, regularly practiced "self-flagellation" to remind her of her sin and how vile she was in the eyes of God. In Islam, Allah tallies up your good deeds and your sins at the end of your life. If you have more sins on your account than good deeds, you go straight to hell. If your good deeds outnumber your sins, even by one tiny little act, you wake up in Paradise. Jewish people have to watch out for the 618 commandments given to them. Violating any of them constitutes sin, and unless they repent, turn back to God, and perform a charitable act, they're in big trouble.

Virtually every religion teaches that if you commit a sin (remember all those lists), God cuts you off until you *do* something to make him welcome you back. It's how I was taught, and if you have any religious background and were raised in the 50s, 60s, or 70s, I'll bet that's how you were taught.

If so, you were taught wrong, and Sister really helped me on this one by giving me a twig.

I really don't like to quote the Bible, because some people who do that are just trying to beat you over the head with it. But this verse from the Gospel of John brilliantly describes how we avoid sin, which we have just learned is separateness: "I am the vine; you are the branches." Perhaps the one message that Sister Camille repeated the most to me was this: "Oh dearie, you're already connected to God, and you always will be!"

She explained that being connected to God—what I prefer to call divine energy—isn't about rules or edicts that someone imposes on you. Instead, it's recognizing that you that this energy is always there, always available. We don't have to do anything or be anything. Sister said that her goal every day was to stay connected to God more often and for longer periods of time.

"Sometimes, dearie, I forget and feel so distant and disconnected, and that's when I need a reminder."

I could hardly believe my ears. If someone as devoted to God as she was could become disconnected, how does someone like me have a chance? We were sitting in Clare Hall, and she reached into a pocket and pulled out a small twig and said, "I want you to carry this with you wherever you go. It will remind you that you are the branch that is always connected to the vine. Always."

To this day, I still carry that twig with me.

"Sister, is everyone connected?" I asked.

"Everyone, dearie."

What about some really bad people who've done awful things," I pressed. "Like the guy that killed Dr. Martin Luther King, Jr. or those people who kidnapped Elizabeth Smart. They can't possibly be connected, can they?

"Yes, even them. The problem is they don't know they are connected. If they had, they never would have done those awful things. And when we forget or ignore the reality that we're connected, we're likely to do things we later regret. Those people are not awful—they simply are not aware of how damaged the connection has gotten between them and God.

Her answer reminded me of a retreat I attended conducted by Ken Blanchard, author of the best-selling book *The One Minute Manager*. He asked us to estimate where we might land on a continuum of total separation to being completely united with God. The number zero would be basically be total alienation, while the number 100 represented a perfect union. He told us that someone as devoted to God as Mother Teresa was likely at ninety-five because a.) no one's perfect and b.) even Mother Teresa might have had a bad thought on occasion. Then he told us that an axe-murderer would come in around one or two, if for no other reason than his mother probably loved him. But here was the part that got my attention.

"Both the axe murderer and Mother Teresa get the same chance at being completely united with God," he announced, much to the surprise of many. After all, how could someone who had done horrible things be even mentioned in the same breath as a saintly woman who had devoted her entire life to working with the poorest of the poor in Calcutta?

"In God's eyes," Ken continued. "We all have an equal chance to get to 100. It's all because of what God has already done, not what we do. The key is that we all have this opportunity, but we don't all exercise it."

What I love about that is that being connected to the vine is available to us all; it may require more exercise for the axe murderer than for Mother Teresa. Consider where you are on that continuum. Maybe you're at seventy-five. On a good day, I might be at eighty. But guess what. I don't have an advantage over you. I may have to be more intentional to get close to God, and yeah, I may have to work harder than Mother Teresa to be as connected to God as she is.

At the same time, the possibility exists that some people never acknowledge that they are connected. They are so dark that they are unable to see the light of God, so the question always comes up, "What happens to them?" The Western way of thinking tells us they go to hell where they experience eternal punishment, but I just don't buy that. To be perfectly honest, I don't know what happens when we die, but I do not believe God or divine energy is capable of such cruelty. And here's where I think the Eastern view makes more sense. It may be that the axe murderer needs to be given another chance at life in the form of reincarnation in order to experience the connection that is always there for us. And hell? A few years ago, I heard someone describe what I believe is the perfect image of hell: an individual sitting all alone in a cave. Complete separation from the Divine. *Time* magazine published a cover story on hell. For the cover, they depicted a person sitting all alone on a rock. I've never gotten that image out of my mind.

While the twig that I carry with me is a helpful reminder that I'm connected, we can still become lost. To keep that from happening, Sister told me, we need to develop a practice to keep us on track. From her example, I bookend my days with prayer and meditation. I practice rituals such as reading Scripture, reciting Franciscan prayers, listening to inspirational tapes from a variety of sources—including the *Tao Te Ching*—slowing down, and centering myself before heading out into the day. I've also created my "Fourteen Stations," which help me stay connected every day (see appendix). Sister counseled that the amount of time we devote to these rituals isn't important. What *is* important, she said, is that we carve out some sacred space every day, so that we remain connected to the vine. I asked her how long it takes hear each day.

"Dearie, do them until you're ready to say yes to the day."

Then at the end of the day, with Sister's help, I developed these eight questions that I ask myself:

1. What's the best thing I experienced today?

2. How did I do today to live my ideal day?

3. What was one new thing that I learned today?

4. How did God work through me today?

5. What am I most grateful for today?

6. What did I do to inspire others?

7. What am I most looking forward to tomorrow?

8. What did I do today to create a belly laugh?

The more Sister and I talked, the more her idea of being connected made sense to me. For example, I had been taught that we need to repent of our sins, but I never really knew what that meant. At least not the way Sister explained it.

Sister said, "The Greek word for repent, metanoia, literally means "change of mind." In other words, whenever I feel as if I'm not connected, I need to change my mind. That little twig in my pocket is one way to remind me of what already exists."

The challenge, then, for all of us is to find ways to remind ourselves that we are indeed connected to God and remain in that mindfulness longer and more often. Religion tries to do that with doctrine, and doctrine ultimately leads to those lists of dos and don'ts. True spirituality offers paths to connectedness through practices. Think of it this way. If a coach wants his basketball team to win the championship, she doesn't hand her players the rule book and tell them to study it. If she did, she might have a team that knows all the rules, but they'll probably lose all their games. Instead, what do coaches do? They require their teams to practice. To get better at making free throws, they have to shoot dozens of free throws—maybe more—at every practice. To be able to handle the ball better, the coach puts them through a variety of ball-handling drills.

I can't recall a single case where the rule book turned a mediocre team into a great one. But the best teams—the best individual athletes—are the ones who practice hard and often. To know that you are connected to God, you have to remind yourself, and you do that with practice.

Here's a little assignment. Jot down two or three ways you can connect to God or a divine energy to begin and end each day. Then for the next week, do them.

What did these rituals teach you about God? About yourself? What would keep you from continuing these practices?

You are always connected. Don't forget.

— 13 —

LEARNING TO LOVE LIKE GOD

When Sister Camille turned 88, I hosted a big party for her at my house. It was Easter Sunday, the place was packed with friends and family, and it was clear that she was enjoying herself. For one thing, I bought a huge birthday cake, and Sister loved a slice of cake. Or two. And I made sure a had a little gin on hand so I could mix her the perfect martini. Since I was the guy who set this celebration up, I spent most of my time making sure everything was just right, so I really didn't get a chance to hang out with her much. But that was okay. I loved seeing her laugh with my friends and family and have such a good time. At some point, I discovered that we had run out of ice, so I snuck out to my car, drove to a convenience store, and bought a couple of bags of ice. By the time I got back, just about everyone had taken off, leaving Sister on the couch, surrounded by my kids and their cousins. An eighty-eight-year-old nun was the center of attention of about a dozen kids in their teens. Not wanting to interrupt, I busied myself in the kitchen, but mostly I was eavesdropping. What could they possibly be talking about?

Social media. That's right. They were showing her who knows what on their cell phones. She was asking questions about Facebook and Twitter. They were doing their best to explain the appeal of communicating with a device instead of face to face. Both seemed pretty interested in each other. I let them go on for several minutes, but since it was getting late, I butted in and asked Sister if she wanted me to take her home.

"Oh no, dearie. I'm having too much fun."

I remember thinking at the time if I would be able to really enjoy hanging out with teenagers when I am in my eighties. I love kids, but they can wear you out after a while. I suppose her years on a university campus engrained in her a genuine interest in young people, but I had also come to know that Sister relished any opportunity to learn something new, and on that night, those teenagers became her teachers. Eventually, I pretty much "rescued" her, and though she protested a bit, we were soon on the way to her home. When I got back to my place, I was ready to hit the sack. The kids were still up, so I walked through the living room and told them goodnight. Like most teenagers, they probably kept at it until the wee hours of the morning, but I had to be at my office the next day. That, plus I wasn't a teenager.

About a week later, my niece called me about something, and after we talked for a while, I thanked her for being so kind to Sister Camille on her birthday.

"It's not like we were trying to be kind," she laughed. "That nun is the coolest person I've ever met!"

Which only goes to prove that coolness has nothing to do with age or looks. Sister looked like an old lady in her eighties, and she wore her habit everywhere, including to her birthday party. Yet she was indeed cool, which I define as someone who seeks out the good in everything and is filled with wonder over every situation in which she finds herself, even with a bunch of teenagers.

I share that story because it demonstrates a quality in Sister that I not only admire but try to emulate. She was truly interested in those kids, not because she was trying to be cool, but because she quite simply loved them.

Legend has it that the great physicist, Albert Einstein, once said, "All I have ever wanted to do is to learn to think like God thinks." Sister and I talked about this soon after her birthday party. and even though I know what Einstein meant, we came to the conclusion that God doesn't think. Sister suggested, "Whatever you want to call God—Divine Energy, Eternal Light, Higher Power—God doesn't think in the way that we humans think. It's an experience of something powerful that flows through us, primarily manifested in love."

While Sister often reminded me that God loves everyone, she also emphasized that the very essence of God is described in the Gospel of John: "God *is* love." When we are connected to God, that love flows through us and into the lives of others. When Sister stayed up late to talk with those teenagers, she was letting the very essence of God flow through her. When my niece claimed that Sister was the coolest person she'd ever met, she was reflecting that same love, or what I call energy or light, that came from God to Sister, to my niece, and back to God in an eternal flow that is available to all.

Whenever we talked about love, Sister liked to poke a little fun at what some people call "unconditional love."

"That's redundant," she would argue. "True love has no conditions. You don't have to do something to earn love."

It was from Sister that I learned about a Bulgarian philosopher named Peter Deunov who identified three types of love: human, spiritual, and divine. Human love, according to Deunov, always varies and always changes. Think of all the times you've fallen in and out of love. Spiritual love varies but never changes. You always love things of the spirit, but sometimes that love ebbs and flows; it's like the love between a mother and a child. Divine love—love that comes from a higher source of energy— never varies and never changes.

By remaining connected to that energy, Sister was more catholic than Catholic. I better explain that so I don't get in trouble with her sisters back at Clare Hall. Of course, Sister was a good Catholic. Not only had she served as president and chancellor of a Catholic University, but she was serious about her personal Catholic practices. She prayed the rosary every day. Prayed the Stations of the Cross. Celebrated Mass every day. Read daily from her Franciscan prayer book. She loved the Catholic church, serving it all her adult life.

But she was also very much a catholic, and that's not a punctuation error. The word "catholic" with a small "c" means universal. Meaning, in my opinion, that all spirituality is God. As a catholic, Sister was able to see God in all religions, even borrowing some of their practices that helped keep her connected. For example, she adopted some of the Buddhist practices such as surrendering, letting go, and getting quiet. That doesn't mean she was Buddhist or even considered becoming Buddhist. If anything, they made her a better Catholic because they helped her focus on the God she loved and served.

We also read together from the *Tao Te Ching,* an ancient Chinese text that has influenced Confucianism and Buddhism. I have all eighty-one verses of this sacred text on my phone, so whenever we met, I would play one of the verses for her, and we would talk about it. I don't recall her ever criticizing it or pointing out to me that it was wrong or misguided. She never said, "But that's Taoism, Joe. I'm not a Taoist." Of course, she wasn't, and I wasn't trying to turn her into one. She had the wisdom and openness to look for the good in this text and discover how it could enrich her own life.

Of the eighty-one verses of the *Tao,* sixteen deal with water and nature. I fondly recall the many times we read those sections, possibly spending more time with these than with any of the other sections. One day we walked to a bluff overlooking Lake Michigan and sat down at a little picnic table and were silent for a few minutes as we took in the serenity of this lake, which can erupt into waves powerful enough to break a giant ore-carrying freighter in two. But on this day, all was still, and we were momentarily mesmerized by the peacefulness and quiet of our little sanctuary by the lake.

I reached into my pocket, pulled out my phone, and began reading verse 41 of the Tao:

> Water is fluid, soft, and yielding. But water will wear away rock, which is rigid and cannot yield. As a rule, whatever is fluid, soft, and yielding will overcome whatever is rigid and hard. This is another paradox: what is soft is strong.

"Oh dearie, that's beautiful."

I scrolled to another section:

> The supreme good is like water,
> which nourishes all things without trying to.

It is content with the low places that people disdain.
Thus it is like the Tao.

In dwelling, live close to the ground.
In thinking, keep to the simple.
In conflict, be fair and generous.
In governing, don't try to control.
In work, do what you enjoy.
In family life, be completely present.

When you are content to be simply yourself
and don't compare or compete,
everybody will respect you.

"Something that beautiful and true could only come from God," she barely whispered.

It was indeed a sacred moment, a manifestation of something we had earlier labeled PLC: the condition of being peaceful, loving, and connected. She wasn't embracing Taoism or privately tiptoeing away from her Catholic faith. So often she had expressed her belief that all knowledge comes from God, and as I shared these passages with her, I could see that she wasn't just trying to humor me or in a passive-aggressive way keep her views to herself. Later she explained how the *Tao Te Ching* teaching about "being content in the low places" echoed the teachings of Saint Francis on humility, as well as the way Jesus preferred to associate with the poor and oppressed.

"As you know, Saint Francis grew up in a wealthy home, but when he connected with God, he gave away his considerable wealth and took a vow of poverty."

That was how she approached any new or unfamiliar concept. Sister modeled for me a unique ability to see not just the good, but the best, in other people and other ideas, and I have to believe that came from her deep and almost constant connection to God. Conversely, it is when we ignore that connection that we feel the need to be right, raising our defenses and creating conflict where it really isn't necessary. As a modern-day saint, Sister Camille had attained a level of spirituality where there was no room in her soul for judgment, criticism, or any negative feeling to any of God's creatures. All have value and are worthy of respect, whether they shared her Catholic faith, were Jews, Muslims, Buddhist, or atheists. All are connected, which meant she was connected to them and therefore could learn from them.

14

GROWING OLD GRACEFULLY

I never thought of Sister Camille as being old. But she was. When I first met her, she was in her mid-sixties. Life expectancy for women in America is around eighty-one. Even back then, she was living on borrowed time. But in all honesty, she never seemed like an old woman to me.

It wasn't that she looked young. She didn't. The wisps of hair that slipped out of her habit were grey. Her almost cherubic face was lined with wrinkles. When we walked together, I had to hold back a little to match her slower gait. If you saw her that first day I entered her office at the university, you would not have thought her as young or middle aged. For the entire time I knew her, Sister Camille was an old nun.

And yet, she just didn't seem old. Of course, I knew she was what we sometimes call a "senior citizen." I wasn't blind. It's just that age was never an issue for her. What I mean by that is that usually when you're with someone in their sixties and seventies and eighties, it's pretty obvious you're with someone in their eighties. Not to be unkind or over-generalize, but a lot of older people really do act their age, and they've certainly earned the right to do so. You know how to tell if a person is old? Listen for the word "nowadays."

I never heard Sister say nowadays. Or back in the day. Or kids these days. Or the good old days. Her best day was today, but she lived as if tomorrow would be better.

You're never supposed to talk to a woman about her weight or her age. I avoided the first but couldn't resist the second. We talked about aging. A lot. Maybe it was because I knew how quickly time flies, and that with a little luck, I'd be looking at eighty someday. It could also have been motivated by the fact that every time we turned on the television, we got bombarded with ads about wrinkle cream, hair restoration, and walk-in bathtubs—our culture seems hell-bent on staying, or at least looking, young. But mostly it was because I couldn't help but notice how much fun she was having despite her age. What was her secret? Why did she always seem so happy or content? If I wanted to be like Sister when I'm eighty, what would I have to do?

I remember the first time I brought up the subject. We were talking about the trend we had both noticed of people approaching middle age who tried to look like teenagers. I'm sure you've seen it. The neighbor lady who looks like the nice mom that she is who begins wearing hoodies and sweatpants with the word "Pink" embroidered on them to church. Or the guy in your office who gets one of those haircuts where it looks like someone deliberately messed up his hair. We both enjoyed a good laugh about this phenomenon, and then I mentioned something about plastic surgery, and her response stunned me.

"Oh dearie, it makes me so sad when I hear about people doing that. Do you know what happens in plastic surgery?"

I thought she was going to describe in graphic detail what actually goes on in the operating room, but before I could answer, she continued.

"They cut out a part of your soul."

Wow!

But think about it. Whenever you alter the way you look, what you're really saying is "I don't like myself." Let's say you're in your forties and you start noticing a few tine "lines" branching out from your eyes. At first it doesn't bother you, but as the years pass, they become more pronounced. And you begin seeing more on your forehead, and you start thinking, "Damn those wrinkles! I don't look like the guy I used to be." Which is absolutely true, but instead of getting all bent out of shape over it, celebrate that wonderful fact. You're *not* the guy you used to be. You're wiser and probably in a better place emotionally and financially than you were when you were twenty. You've earned those wrinkles from swimming at the beach with your kids, laughing with your buddies until your sides hurt, jogging with your wife on those crisp winter mornings, and sitting in the bleachers at your daughter's softball game. In other words, you've lived a lot, learned a lot, experienced a lot, and even if your face looks like a baseball mitt run over by a truck tire—which it probably doesn't—so what? It's who you are. Why would you want to erase or remove any part of you, whether it's your body, soul, or mind? Get over your vain self and enjoy being you, wrinkles and all.

As that great "philosopher" Jimmy Buffet once observed, "Wrinkles are only places where your smiles have been, so why would you try to hide them?"

Sister Camille wasn't glamorous. She was stout. Always wore a nun's habit. And ah yes, those wrinkles. But because she was so comfortable with who she was, I always thought of her as beautiful. She carried herself with grace and confidence, which is kind of ironic, because you know one of the first things they teach young women who want to become supermodels? Confidence. Not how to apply your make up or wear your hair. Confidence. No one had to teach that to Sister. She regularly hobnobbed with people who spent fortunes trying to look young and beautiful, but she was usually the center of attention.

We returned to the subject of aging so much, that I think I've been able to identify those traits or qualities that enabled Sister to transcend age, which isn't the same as trying to be young. Rather, it's the ability of a person to grow older without letting age define him or her. It really relegates age to being simply a number instead a reason to panic. From the day we're born, we're all aging. So how do we do it gracefully. Consider these characteristics of Sister.

GRATITUDE

I have a friend who meets a group of guys for coffee every Saturday. Most of the men are retired, but a few are in their mid-fifties to early sixties. He told me the one big difference between the retirees and the working stiffs was that the older men were constantly complaining. About everything. The government. The weather. Taxes. Kids who are always looking at their cell phones. The media. Gas prices. Bring up any subject, he said, and they could complain about it.

I never heard Sister complain, even though I'm sure she had plenty of reasons to. You don't run a university or lead a civic organization without running into a lot of annoying interference. It wasn't just that she never complained; she had a mindset of gratitude. She found ways to be grateful for everything, beginning with food. The first time we shared a meal together, she bowed her head and offered a prayer of thanksgiving for the food we were about to eat. The next time, same thing. I wasn't unfamiliar with the practice of saying a quick prayer before a meal, but it seemed like one of those empty rituals we all do. When I asked her about it during one of our restaurant dates, her answer really surprised me.

"Have you ever noticed how much better food tastes after you pray?" she smiled.

We were both working on a wonderfully prepared sirloin steak, and it tasted great. Who am I to argue?

During another meal, she ordered a bowl of fresh fruit. When the server brought it to her, she again prayed, and then held a strawberry up with her fork.

"Isn't this beautiful, dearie? Just think, someone planted a little seed in the ground, someone else came along and watered it, maybe sprinkled some fertilizer on it. If weeds threatened to choke the little strawberry plant, someone pulled the weeds or drove a cultivator down the rows. Finally, when it was just the right time, yet another person carefully picked this exact strawberry. It was washed, packaged and shipped to the market where the chef likely bought it early this morning. All that just so I could enjoy it. Isn't that just wonderful?"

To this day, I can't eat a strawberry and not be grateful to all that went into providing it for my enjoyment.

She didn't stop with the food. One time, as she unwrapped her silverware from the linen napkin during one of our lunches, she asked me if I had ever really looked at the knives and spoons and forks with which I eat my food.

"Somebody mined the metal used to make these, and another person melted it down and poured it into a mold. After it cooled, yet another individual polished it, removing any imperfections and giving you and me these beautiful utensils to use as we enjoy our meal."

She was like this about most things in her life—genuinely thankful for everything from the air we breathed, to the students she got to know, even the challenges of running a university.

"Gratitude changes your mindset about everything," she once told me. "You can complain about your job, or you can be thankful you *have* a job. When you look at it that way, it literally turns your job into blessing."

Incidentally, she never retired. She once told me that the definition of retire is to withdraw, fade away, or become less significant. Who would sign up for that? She was grateful for work and always found a way to *refire* her life rather than retire.

FORGIVENESS

Over the years, I became aware of a few occasions where people either took advantage of Sister or treated her unfairly, yet I've never seen her get angry or upset about it. Whenever I learned about those things, I wanted to go settle the score, but she wisely counseled me that there was nothing to settle. Carrying a grudge just wasn't on her agenda.

"Forgiveness is a lot easier when we stop and consider all the times we've needed to be forgiven," she counseled. "Besides, people who forgive tend to live longer."

I'm not sure if that's true, but when a ninety-year old makes that claim, you tend to believe them.

I wish I could say that whenever I had been mistreated, I turned the other cheek and offered my forgiveness. The truth is, I once held a grudge against a former business partner for fifteen years. The details aren't important. Let's just say the proper business term for what he did to me was this: he screwed me. Big time. I not only let him know what I thought of him, but whenever I would see him around town, I'd turn my back and walk away from him. For fifteen years!

In one of our more "confessional" times together, I decided to come clean with Sister, maybe secretly hoping she would understand and even approve of my long-term grudge. Good luck with that.

"What do you hope to accomplish with all this, dearie?"

"Sister, it's just my way of getting revenge. After all, I trusted him even as he was going behind my back and spreading lies about me to my clients. Then he stole those clients from me. The guy cost me hundreds of thousands of dollars in lost revenue."

"Well dearie, if it's revenge you're after, you need to go buy a shovel."

"Huh?"

"Because you'll have to dig two graves—one for him and one for you. You've got to let it go dearie."

Not exactly what I wanted to hear from her, but I knew she was right. Carrying a grudge around is hard work, and I can't say it made me feel better. Maybe for a couple of seconds after walking away from him I felt like I was giving him major payback. But deep down inside, I felt pretty small. Sister helped give me the courage to do what I knew I had to do. I first went on a spiritual retreat and, at Sister's urging, centered my thoughts on surrounding the guy with light and love. I spent the entire two days thinking about him and my behavior and how I could release the negative thoughts I had about him. I even prayed for an opportunity to meet with him, and as they say, "Be careful what you pray for."

After not seeing him for about two years, upon returning from my spiritual retreat, I ran into him at some social event in the city. I knew that his favorite drink was a "7&7," so I hustled over to the cash bar, bought a couple, walked across the ballroom and handed him a drink.

"Why thanks, Joe!"

That's all it took. We chatted for a while, and I told him that what he did those many years ago really hurt me, but that I forgave him. And that I was sorry for the way I handled it. Now, whenever he sees me, he gives me a big hug. But the best part of this story is that I no longer carry around the burden of vengeance toward another human being. Sister helped me understand that my lack of forgiveness was hurting me more than it hurt him. And by observing her endure her own injustices, I gained insight into how to grow old gracefully.

SIMPLICITY

Sister Camille didn't own a lot of stuff. Compare that to the fact that one in eleven Americans pays $91.14 per month for self-storage units to keep all the junk that won't fit in their 2,000 square foot homes because the attic, basement, garage, and closets are stuffed. Currently, we're filling 2.3 billion square feet of self-storage space in the United States.

Sister shared a modest house with her sister, and when she eventually moved into Clare Hall after her sister's death, she didn't need a huge estate sale to get rid of things. I'm sure part of the reason Sister Camille lived such a simple life was due to the teachings of her beloved Saint Francis, as well as the Franciscan order to which she belonged. But I think she also realized that the more stuff you have the more those things tend to possess you, robbing you of what really gives you joy in life. You buy that big boat because, well, you can. But then you feel you have to get out on it every weekend because of how much it cost. Then there's all the work and expense of upkeep. Your kids would much rather go to the park and play a pick-up game of basketball, but you drag them to the marina instead. This may not apply to you, but substitute the word "boat" with country club, cabin in the mountains, time-share in Florida, motorhome, etc. Nothing wrong with any of those things, but they generally do not deliver all that you thought they would.

Sister had her friends, the Franciscans, her beloved Packers, and her occasional indulgence in a good meal preceded by a martini. What else did she need? She could get as much enjoyment from the rabbits and birds in her yard as she did from a hefty donation to her university.

HUMOR

So many times, Sister stated what was obvious in her attitude and demeanor: humor is good for the soul. The reason why, she said, is that it detaches us from situations we face and keeps us from taking ourselves too seriously. She loved a good laugh, like the one she had with her dear friend, Cardinal Timothy Dolan, who served as archbishop in Milwaukee for eight years. At a dinner following Dolan's appointment to New York as a Cardinal, Sister asked him how it felt to be a Cardinal. A rabid baseball fan, Dolan replied, "Sister, the only cardinal I ever wanted to be was Stan Musial, the greatest St. Louis Cardinal ever." To which Sister replied, "Well now that you're going to New York, you have a problem. Are you going to be a Met or a Yankee?"

His answer sent her into stitches:

"Forgive me Sister, but that's one issue where I'm pro-choice."

Thanks to Sister and Cardinal Dolan, I've now added an eighth question to my daily Seven Questions, and that's "What did I do today to create a belly laugh for myself and others."

WISDOM

Albert Einstein once observed that "Wisdom is not a product of schooling, but a lifelong attempt to acquire it." Sister was extremely intelligent, but she was also wise. Her years of study gave her mastery of a body of knowledge that helped her succeed at every position she held at the university. But it was her "supplemental education" as a student of life that made her wise. She could go toe-to-toe with anyone when it came to discussions of policy, budgets, strategic planning, and the like. At the same time, she could stop a meeting in its tracks with an insightful comment that took the discussion to a whole new level and usually left everyone going, "Whoa!"

I experienced those "whoa" moments often with Sister Camille. One time during a meal, we somehow got on the subject of optimism, and I said something like "He's a glass half-full kind of guy."

Sister paused for a moment, then pointed to the glass of water sitting next to her plate."

"Dearie, is that glass half full or half empty?"

I thought she was trying to determine if I was an optimist or a pessimist, so I answered in what I felt was both honest and helpful."

"To me, Sister, it's half full."

Generally, I'm pretty optimistic about things and thought my answer would satisfy her.

"No, dearie, it's neither," she answered, and now I was totally confused.

"That glass is completely perfect. What do we all need?

The puzzled look on my face must have told her I didn't have a clue what she was getting at.

"Half the glass is water, half is air. We need both to live. It's perfect, just as it is."

That's just the way she thought. Intelligence tells us that the glass is either half full or half empty. Wisdom tells us that life isn't always an either/or proposition, that what appears to be one thing is actually another. Perfect.

She was ninety-three when she shared that nugget of wisdom with me.

Compared to Sister, I'm still a pretty young guy. But I know that with passing year, I'm getting older. I'm not really afraid of dying, which I'll explain soon, but you know what really scares me? Turning into a grumpy old man. Spending my "golden years" complaining about today and wishing I could go back to the good old days, which we all know weren't really that great. Thanks to Sister Camille's example, I can't wait to hit ninety.

Because life really does get better if we learn to grow old gracefully.

15

IT'S IN GIVING THAT WE RECEIVE

I've never been much of a drinker. I'll enjoy a beer now and then, but if you see me cracking open a second bottle, you'll know I've decided to liver dangerously (that's not a typo). I'm just not that guy who gets shitfaced at every party. A lot of that probably has to do with the fact that I've had friends and family that struggled with alcoholism. Watching people you love lose so much because of alcohol is a pretty good deterrent. But I've also seen occasional drinkers make the mistake of taking that second cocktail, only to do something silly that they regretted later. All that to say one of the highlights in my relationship with Sister Camille occurred after I unwisely and uncharacteristically ordered a second drink after an especially long fundraiser with Sister.

"Sister Camille, what's one thing you'd like to do before you die?"

She was eighty-eight at the time, and no way would I have been so bold or imprudent to ask such a question were it not for the extra ounce of alcohol.

Sister didn't miss a beat.

"Oh dearie, I'd love to meet Barbara Bush again," she volunteered. "You know, she spoke at our commencement thirty-five years ago, and I've followed her ever since. She's such a remarkable woman. I'm pretty sure I'm one of millions who'd like to meet her, but you asked."

Sharing a martini with Sister. This libation led to a conversation about the quality days she had remaining.

Indeed, I did, and now I felt even worse. In my slightly inebriated condition, I not only reminded her of her impending mortality, but planted the tiniest seed of possibility in her mind. As impossible as it seemed, I knew I had to at least try. But once again, the gin began to talk.

"Well Sister, I'm going to try and make this happen, and I'll start first thing tomorrow morning!"

Have you ever had one of those "I knew what I was feeling, but what was I thinking" moments? That was one of them for me. How in the hell was I going to arrange for an eighty-eight-year old nun to meet the former First Lady of the United States? Both Mrs. Bush and her husband were getting up in years themselves, so I knew I had to act fast. Then it hit me like a two-by-four up the side of my head: "You wrote a book about networking; maybe you oughta practice what you preach!"

Duh.

I began flipping through my mental contact list and landed on the name of John McConnell, an attorney who used to write speeches for both President George W. Bush and Vice President Dick Cheney. I called him and asked if he could put me in touch with anyone in President Bush's circle and was thrilled when he offered the email address for Hutton Heston, Mrs. Bush's personal assistant.

I contacted Hutton, explaining how Sister Camille met Mrs. Bush several years ago and had followed her and her husband over the years, then made my request: would it be possible for Sister Camille to have lunch with President and Mrs. Bush?

Although I'm an optimist by nature, I pretty much expected a polite decline. After all, he probably gets hundreds of such requests a day. At least I could report back to Sister that I had tried. And then I got the response from Hutton: "Barbara has fond memories of Sister, and she'd be open to the possibility of doing lunch."

Of course, I was thrilled. I immediately suggested that Sister Camille could fly to Houston, where the Bushes lived and asked for a date that fit their busy schedules, only to hear back from Hutton that President and Mrs. Bush would be at their family compound in Kennebunkport, Maine for the next six months. We're talking about people in their late eighties and nineties. A lot could happen during that time, and I didn't want to wait. So, I took a deep breath and asked if Sister Camille could meet them at Kennebunkport instead of Houston, and Hutton graciously agreed.

For some reason, my geography placed Kennebunkport just outside Boston and began looking into commercial flights from Milwaukee to Boston. Bad geography. The Bush family compound is a good hundred miles from Boston. The logistics of getting a 88 year-old nun from Logan International to Kennebunkport seemed a little dicey, so I began looking into the possibility of chartering a private jet, which took me to another contact in my network: Chris Doerr.

Chris owned Sterling Aviation, a charter aircraft company. We'd done business together and, in the process, became good friends. I called to share my need for a charter flight to Kennebunkport.

"Kennebunkport," he exclaimed. "What have you got going on out there?

I really didn't want to name drop, but I sort of mumbled, "I'm part of a meeting with President and Mrs. Bush." To say that got his attention is the understatement of the century.

"Oh, *just* a little meeting with the President and his wife, huh?"

Realizing that I may have made it sound like it was all about me, I explained that the *real* reason for the trip was to facilitate a meeting between the Bushes and Sister Camille.

"Sister Camille from Cardinal Stritch," he exclaimed. "I love that woman!"

So far, so good.

"Chris, you know I've never asked you for anything. I don't have a lot of money. Is there any way we could use one of your planes if I paid for maybe the pilot and the fuel? Maybe, we could also get you a tax deduction from Cardinal Stritch."

"Joe, if you're going to meet the president, you should take my Challenger 300," he responded.

I knew a little about that fantastic aircraft. Made by Bombardier, this $30 million baby cruises at around 550 miles per hour with a range of 3,200 miles. It could easily get us to Kennebunkport and back on a single tank of gas. I'd also done some research and learned that chartering a Challenger runs around $8,000 per hour. To fly to Kennebunkport, have a brief lunch, and then fly back could probably be done in five or six hours. That's at least $50,000, about $48,000 more than I could afford.

"Chris, I know what you charge to charter that plane, and it's more than I was planning to spend. Any way you can cut me a deal?"

I really meant that as a joke, because even if he cut his price in half, I still wouldn't be able to come up with that kind of money. His answer was as unexpected as it was outrageous.

"Joe, if you take me along as your wingman, I'll fly you and Sister out for free."

Once again, I could hardly believe my ears; once again, reality hit like a sledgehammer. I had just promised to get this guy into the Bush family compound without clearing it with the Secret Service. Mrs. Bush's assistant, Hutton Heston, had gotten security clearance through the Secret Service for Sister and me. Slipping another guy through the gate presented yet another challenge. I just hoped that Sister would approve of my, shall we say, divine deception.

Boarding the private jet to Kennibunkport to visit the Bushes

I got in touch with my contact person at the Secret Service and talked as fast as I could.

"You see, this distinguished Catholic nun who President and Mrs. Bush love dearly is 88 years old and a little unsteady on her feet. I can assist her on one side, but I really need someone else to help on her other side, and I was able to talk the pilot of my private jet to share that responsibility with me."

Silence.

"Okay. Here's the deal. He's giving us the plane for free, and I promised he could go in with us."

I hope I don't get anyone in trouble, but the Secret Service guy laughed and said, "Your guy is cleared. Enjoy your visit."

Things were really falling into place. I thought it would be nice to present Camille and Mrs. Bush with a bouquet of flowers and stopped at a florist before we had to head to the Milwaukee airport. When I asked the manager to show me some samples, he asked me who I was giving the flowers to.

"Barbara Bush and Sister Camille," I answered, trying to sound as nonchalant as I could, but he couldn't hide his enthusiasm.

"Sister Camille?" he exclaimed. "The lady who used to be the president of Cardinal Stritch?"

When I assured him that's who would be getting one of the bouquets, he said, "I've got just the perfect arrangement for you."

He walked into the back room and emerged a few seconds later carrying the most beautiful arrangement of flowers I'd ever seen in my life. He told me they were Freedom Roses, the classic red rose, but a special variety grown in the volcanic soil of Ecuador. Each arrangement had about two dozen of those beautiful flowers; he was right—they were perfect for the occasion, and I wasn't going to let the $130 per arrangement bother me. But when I reached for my wallet, he stopped me.

"These are on me."

The day finally arrived, and we boarded Chris's luxurious jet. After a pleasant flight of just under two hours, we landed at a nearby commuter airport, climbed into a waiting shuttle van, and within minutes were standing at the front door of the Bushes lovely getaway overlooking the Atlantic Ocean. As I looked for a doorbell, the door swung open and there she was—the unmistakable smiling face and snow-white hair.

"Welcome Sister!" she exclaimed, and the two embraced as if they were old friends.

Mrs. Bush ushered us into her home and gave us a quick tour of the first floor that ended in the living room where her husband greeted us. When she asked us if we'd like something to drink, I requested some iced tea.

"The President doesn't like to drink alone," she frowned. "Could I interest you in a glass of white wine?"

In a few moments, I was sitting right next to the forty-first president of the United States, sipping a glass of wine, and chatting as easily with him as if he was one of my buddies back in Milwaukee. For some reason I asked him if he had seen President Clinton lately.

"Bubba? He was out here last week."

Then Mrs. Bush interrupted from across the room.

"Bill Clinton is the smartest guy I've ever met. He could tell you in one breath how to solve a major international problem and in the next, how to hunt ducks in Arkansas. You couldn't shut him up. He talked for four hours straight, but I feel sorry for him. He also appears to be one of the loneliest men I have met."

I just sat there taking it all in as President Bush continued about his friend, Bill Clinton.

"While he was out here visiting, I asked him where he'd like to go for dinner. We have this marvelous restaurant in Kennebunkport called Stripers, but he kept asking me, 'When are we going to Strippers?'" The Bushes and Clintons were political enemies for decades and transformed that relationship to become political allies. Is there something we can all learn from the Bushes and the Clintons?

It was almost surreal. I say almost because truthfully, despite his life of distinguished service to our nation including holding the most powerful office in the world, President Bush really seemed like a regular guy. He seemed as genuinely interested in us as we were in him. When he talked, his eyes sparkled, and he leaned forward as if to say, "You guys are all right."

After a few minutes of delightful conversation, a housekeeper entered the living room and announced that lunch was about to be served. As I approached the table, I couldn't help but wonder how many world leaders, members of congress, cabinet members, and Bush family members had gathered around this same table. Pretty heady stuff. I was doing okay until the First Lady asked Sister Camille to say grace,s and we all held hands as she began. As she began in her steady voice began to thank God for the food and bless and protect the President and Mrs. Bush, I couldn't hold back the tears. It didn't help much when I peeked over at the president and saw a couple of tears streaming down his ruddy cheeks. I glanced over at Chris, and even he was wiping his eyes.

When she finished praying, Mrs. Bush, who by then had insisted I call her Barbara, turned our tears into laughter.

"What's everyone crying for?"

The lunch was simple yet elegant: lobster salad, rolls fresh out of the oven, ice cream for dessert. But again, it was almost as if I was back in my own home with friends sharing a meal and getting caught up. Regardless of your politics, if you ever would have had the privilege of meeting President and Mrs. Bush, you would be just as disarmed as I was by their decency and grace. They really were wonderful hosts.

Sister Camille and Barbara Bush reunited after 30 years

Too soon it was time to leave. We said our goodbyes and then headed back to the little airport and boarded the jet, and that's when the fun began. As we climbed to around 39,000 feet, I reached into my pocket and pulled out a paper napkin with the presidential seal that I had swiped. Then Chris, not to be outdone, showed us that he had similarly slipped one of those napkins into his own pocket and proudly displayed it.

"Oh boys, that's nothing," Sister Camille chuckled as she sipped the largest martini I had ever seen, and reached into her purse, pulling out a large paper towel with the Walker's Point logo on it.

I didn't ask, but I secretly entertained the idea of my deeply spiritual friend visiting the rest room and spying a stack of those towels on the countertop. Wise woman that she was, she probably knew that security cameras were hidden all over the place. Except for the restrooms. Regardless, we all enjoyed a great laugh over our shenanigans, and like elementary-school kids riding the bus home from their first day of school, we replayed all our wonderful memories all the way back to Milwaukee. It didn't hurt that Chris stashed a bottle of gin and two huge martini glasses in one of the storage bins.

Sister with her favorite martini, extra large to celebrate a special day.

It turns out we didn't have to steal our little souvenirs. In all the excitement of our visit, I had forgotten that someone pulled us all together for a group picture. A few days after we returned, I received a large envelope in the mail and, noting the return address, quickly but carefully opened it. There we were: Chris, the First Lady, President Bush, Sister Camille, and me. Beneath the photo, this caption: "In gratitude for sharing a most memorable day with President George H. W. Bush and First Lady Barbara Bush" followed by both their signatures. I learned later that both Chris and Sister received the same treasured memento. What a classy couple.

Photo sent to us by President Bush along with a heartfelt handwritten
note thanking us for coming to visit with them.

A few days after this incredible experience, Sister asked me to stop by her
house on my way home from work. She had remembered it was my birthday
and had a card for me. She wanted to make sure I got it right on my birthday,
not a couple of days later in the mail. I pulled into her driveway, and before I
could get to the front door, she came out, gave me a little hug, then handed
me an envelope.

"Thank you again dearie for all you did to arrange that remarkable visit with the Bushes. What can I do for you?"

I can't tell you how many times I'd heard her ask that same question to me and so many others.

"Absolutely nothing, Sister. I don't need a thing. It was a gift just to share that experience with you."

But she persisted, and I realized that she was practicing something both of us had talked about many times: if you can help other people get what you want, you can do things you never imagined possible. That's exactly how we were able to go to Kennebunkport. I helped her realize an impossible dream of hers and by doing that was able to do something I never thought I could ever do. Now she wanted to give back. So, I went for it.

"Sister, you know how much I love to have you pray the Prayer of St. Francis with me. It would be an honor if you could pray it with me every day."

I pulled out my phone and tapped the video recorder icon.

"Would you be willing to pray that prayer into my recorder, so that I can watch and listen to you pray that every day for the rest of my life?"

"Why of course, dearie."

There in her prayer room, sitting in her meditation chair she began in a soft, reverent voice:

> Lord, make me an instrument of Thy peace;
> Where there is hatred, let me sow love;
> Where there is injury, pardon;
> Where there is doubt, the faith;
> Where there is despair, hope;
> Where there is darkness, light;
> And where there is sadness, joy.

O Divine Master, grant that I may not so much seek to be consoled as to console; to be understood as to understand; to be loved as to love.

For it is in giving that we receive; it is in pardoning that we are pardoned, and it is in dying that we are born to eternal life.

Amen.

16

A GRACE-FILLED LIFE

One of the most popular hymns sung or played at funerals is "Amazing Grace." Penned by John Newton, a slave-trader who was caught in a violent storm off the coast of County Donegal, Ireland. The waves were so severe that he feared for his life and called out to God for mercy. This marked his spiritual conversion, and a few years later he wrote this popular hymn to provide support for a New Year's Day sermon. It's message of forgiveness and redemption has drawn millions to change the trajectory of their lives from being "lost" in their own selfishness to being "found" by God. Or as I might reframe it, recognizing that we are already connected to God or the Divine Energy. Newton spent the rest of his life freeing slaves.

Whenever I think of this amazing grace, I think of Sister Camille. If I could choose one word to describe her, it would be grace. She lived a grace-filled life. Even more accurately, she reflected something called "grace light," which is the light of God. It is invisible to most, but visible to sages and highly evolved people. Grace light is filled with a higher intelligence, a higher power, and it will transform you in mind, body, and spirit. You saw this grace light in Sister Camille. The beauty of her is that grace light from her was seen and witnessed by almost everyone. The dictionary defines grace as "simple elegance" and "courteous goodwill." They could have been describing Sister. But where did this elegance come from? How was she able to live such a grace-filled life? I believe the answer lies in her beloved St. Francis and St. Clare, and specifically in the famous prayer that is attributed to St. Francis. She not only prayed this prayer every day of her life, she lived it. Here's how:

Lord, make me an instrument of thy peace

She often interchanged the words "make me a channel of your love and peace." Most people desire peace in their hearts or lives; Sister lived to bring peace to others. I think that's what made her such an effective leader. She had the gift of being able to diffuse tense situations, not with words so much as by her example. She lived the Franciscan philosophy. *Preach the gospel always. When necessary use words.* Sister never asked for peace—simply make me a channel for God's peace.

Where there is hatred, let me sow love

In three-plus decades of knowing Sister, I never once heard her say a single negative word about anything. The only time she got grumpy was when the Packers lost. It wasn't that she didn't run into trouble or didn't face any difficult challenges in her life. She just had an uncanny ability to reframe everything in a positive light. For example, most people complain when it rains, but she would often say things like "Isn't it great that the rain comes and cleans everything up. Take a deep breath, Joe. Breathe in the flowers, the grass, and the earth in all of its raw beauty." She told me once that if we have the choice to be right or to be kind, always choose kindness.

Where there is injury, pardon

Sister Camille tried to heal the wounds of the injured, of the sad people who needed her guidance in their lives. A freshman who was lost, homesick. I watched her hug students as she walked across the campus. A faculty member whose father had passed. She was never the kind of leader who used fear and intimidation to get results. Her direct reports knew they worked for someone who believed in second chances, and that encouraged them to be innovative, creative.

Where there is doubt, the faith

We talked a lot about doubt. "Doubt and fear are not of God," she counseled many times. At the same time, she never criticized me when I expressed my doubts, never tried to correct me. Rather, she encouraged me to pursue my questions regarding faith with honesty and openness. She believed that anyone who truly seeks God will find him/her.

Where there is despair, hope

One of the few actual arguments we had was over a verse in the Bible that looks at faith, hope, and love and teaches that of those three, love is the greatest. "No, it's not!" she sternly countered. "The greatest of those is hope." She went on to explain that when people are depressed or in a desperate situation, they don't need to hear someone say, "I love you." What they need more than anything is hope, the belief that they can make it; they can get through their tough times. Faith and love are important, but when you are facing despair, you need hope, and Sister lived her life in such a way as to offer hope to the hopeless.

Where there is darkness, light

When Sister walked into a room, you could almost see the room brighten. She had this aura about her that was unmistakable. I saw it the very first time I met her. I knew immediately that she was someone special, and it had nothing to do with her position as president of a university. I mentioned this to her once, and as you might expect, she took no credit for her uplifting demeanor. "I pray every day that God will let his light flow through me and into others."

And where there is sadness, joy

Sister Camille was quick to laugh. She enjoyed a good joke, both telling them and hearing them. But she also emphasized the difference between happiness and joy. Happiness is usually dependent on circumstances. You're happy when surrounded by friends and family, maybe a little sad or morose when they leave. But joy could be present in both situations. For Sister, joy was an emotion that we feel when we are connected to God and let his light shine through us. This enabled her to feel joy even when things didn't turn out as she had planned.

Grant that I may not so much seek to be consoled as to console

Sister often remarked, "It's not about me; it's about others." You might say that one of her titles was "Chief Consolation Officer." Not just at the university, but in her neighborhood and on the boards and committees she served. She had an innate ability to sense who in her path was having a bad day or going through a difficult time, then offer just the right words or acts of encouragement. On my numerous walks with her on the campus of Cardinal Stritch University, I saw her literally dozens of times excuse herself to go counsel someone that she knew had recently lost a parent, flunked an exam, or was struggling with a personal issue.

To be understood as to understand

For nearly three decades, I threw a lot of wacky ideas at Sister, many that on the surface, at least, directly challenged or even countered her treasured Catholic faith. I always knew when she didn't quite buy what I was selling because of her trademark response: "Help me understand." And it wasn't just a ploy to buy some time, so she could come up with a better argument to put me in my place. She really wanted to know why I believed the way I did, and it wasn't just me. I saw her do that over and over with people who challenged her.

To be loved as to love

Sister Camille practiced unconditional love for everybody. Not just the "good" people in her life. Everyone. We talked about this a lot, and occasionally I would challenge her. "What about the terrorists who crashed two planes into the World Trade Center?" She didn't hesitate. "Of course, I don't approve of what they did. It was awful. But they are children of God as much as I am, and I am called to love them." She often recited from the Sermon on the Mount, "Love your enemies, bless those who curse you, do good to those who hate you, and pray for those who spitefully use you and persecute you." These were not mere words she quoted so that she looked "spiritual." She lived them.

For it is giving that we receive

As a Franciscan nun, Sister Camille did not have many earthly possessions. She didn't need much. Yet she was one of the most generous people I've ever known. It was from her that I discovered a slightly different take on this section of the prayer. Many people think it means if we want to get more stuff, we need to give more money to the church. It's called the "prosperity gospel," and is used by a lot of TV preachers to raise money. But what this really means is that when you give, you realize you don't need as much, to the point that even the smallest gift is a blessing. On our walks she would occasionally see a penny or a dime on the sidewalk. Most of us don't even notice things like that, let alone stoop to pick it up. But Sister always stopped, picked up the coin, and prayed, "Thank you God for the abundance in my life."

It is in pardoning that we are pardoned

Sister never held a grudge, even though there were many occasions when most of us would say she had every right to. On one occasion when I came back from a consulting gig with the Navy SEALs, proudly wearing a SEAL T-shirt that read, "It's not our job to judge whether the terrorists are good or bad. That's God's job. Our job is to set up the meeting." I thought that was pretty cool, but Sister did not approve. "Oh dearie, even terrorists need to be pardoned."

And it is in dying that we are born to eternal life

Sister never expressed fear of dying. That's because she knew that physical death opened the door to eternal life with her God. In a way, she died every day—to herself, her ego, ambitions and desires that would block the flow of light, preventing it from flowing through her and into others. Her life was a resounding affirmation of the oft-quoted John Donne verse, "Oh death, where is thy sting?"

You might think that hanging out with such a deeply spiritual woman left me feeling as if I could never measure up, but it was specifically because she lived such a grace-filled life that I began to see that the divine energy that she tapped into regularly is available to every one of us. I'm no modern-day saint but learning from Sister Camille has clearly made me a better person. It's not a magic formula or some spooky ideology, but a life so connected to God that we can't help but be changed. Are you interested?

Here's your assignment. Pray this prayer every day for the next thirty days. But don't just pray it, do your best to live it. At first it will seem impossible. Forgive that jerk who went behind my back? Hey, the world's a dark place—how is my little light going to change anything? How can I love that guy who shot all those kids at their school? Just keep praying and looking for ways to turn your prayer into action. Start with the little things. You may not be able to forgive a terrorist, but can you forgive your son for coming home drunk. Sure, you can (just try to remember when you were his age). Can you smile a little more instead of acting as if you have the weight of the world on your shoulders (you don't). Can you be that person who, when everyone else says it will never work, says "Hey, let's not give up so easily. We can do it!"

Those small steps turn into bigger ones and though you—or I—may never become a modern-day saint like Sister Camille, we'll gradually free ourselves from the forces that keep us from becoming a channel for the Light to shine through us.

Even in the face of sadness and death.

17

WE NEVER DIE

Shortly after my mom died, I began volunteering for an organization that provided hospice services and palliative care. Mom spent her final days in hospice, and I just thought everyone connected with the program had this aura about them. Even though they had not known my mom, they demonstrated such love and concern for her. I thought to myself, I've gotta do this.

If you're not familiar with hospice, it's where a person who is seriously ill has reached a point where recovery is not possible. Rather than continuing with heroic (and expensive) measures that may actually create more pain and suffering with little to no hope of curing the illness, the patient is placed in a comfortable environment—preferably his or her home—and allowed to pass with dignity, surrounded by friends and family and tended to regularly by volunteers trained in hospice care. I took the training and over time was assigned to about five or six people who were close to the end of their lives.

Then when Sister Camille moved from her home to Clare Hall, joining about sixty-five other elderly nuns in the convent, I cut back on my work with hospice, reasoning that I could be more helpful by checking in regularly with the nuns, all who were elderly with time running out on their earthly journey. It also gave me an excuse to continue hanging out with Sister. So, about every week or ten days, I headed over to Clare Hall, sometimes to join them for a meal (and deliver the cases of wine that they enjoyed so much). Sometimes only for a quick visit to say hello and check in with Sister Camille. But always feeling that I had received more from them than I gave,

Not too long after she moved into Clare Hall, Sister had a small stroke, which for someone her age, could be fatal. I honestly thought she was going to die. Remarkably, she recovered quickly, and at ninety-years-old, the only noticeable damage being a slight speech impediment. But through therapy, she soon regained her ability to speak clearly, yet this fairly serious health crisis got my attention. Sister Camille isn't going to live forever. By then, we were so close that I knew we could talk about anything, so I began asking her about death and dying, and as you might imagine, she was open and honest about her thoughts. She was ninety-two years old. She knew every day was a gift. She loved life, yet she never expressed fear or sadness about death. I wanted to know why.

Think about that for a moment. Over the years I've made the mistake of bringing up the subject of death with friends or family members, and the responses were always the same: "Why do you want to talk about something so morbid?" "Can we please change the subject?" "You're such a downer." It's kind of funny in a way. Every one of us is going to experience death someday, but no one wants to talk about it. Yet with Sister, we could talk about it for hours. And we did, on many occasions.

Even back when I was a kid, I was interested in this somewhat taboo subject. It wasn't taboo to me, and maybe we can learn something from that. I've found that kids, perhaps in their innocence, have no problem talking about death. Next time you're at a funeral, look at the adults, then look at the kids. The adults are all morose and speaking in hushed tones. The kids are running around, laughing (until Mom or Dad collars them). And if you talk to them, they're usually pretty forthcoming: "Nana's in heaven now. I'll bet she's having fun." "Poppa loved to fish. Do you think he's fishing in heaven?" It's only after adults condition them to be afraid of death that they begin to clam up about it. How sad. Well I thought about it a lot, and when I was about seven or eight years old, I asked my dad what happens to us when we die. I got the expected answer from my never-miss-Mass dad: "We either go to heaven or hell." That just didn't cut it with me. All I could think was "That's it?" It made me think how sad it was that when a baby dies; it's all over. A year or so on the planet, and then she's gone? Never made sense to me.

Then in college, I had the privilege of hearing Elisabeth Kübler-Ross speak. At the time, she was a pioneer in the subject of death and dying, and her 1969 groundbreaking book, *On Death and Dying,* remains a classic to this day. It was from her that I learned the five stages of grief that accompany terminal illness: denial, anger, bargaining, depression, and acceptance. They made sense at the time but became real for me as I volunteered for hospice.

Of course, over the years I've had friends and family members die, but death became intimately close to me with my experience with regression analysis when I was hypnotized and asked to report what I saw in my past. After it was all over, one of the questions my counselor asked me was "What did you think when you first returned to the present?" I didn't hesitate for a second because I clearly remember my firth thoughts: "Wow! Life is so short. I was born. Went to school. Joined the Army. And died."

Sister's stroke and my mom's death rekindled my interest in death and dying, and I began reading and studying everything I could get my hands on about the topic. Two great books stand out: Anita Moorjani's *Dying to Be Me,* and Eugene Kelly's *Chasing Daylight—How My Forthcoming Death Changed My Life.* I read these books back-to-back, and they blew me away. She died and came back in a near death experience. He was a fifty-three-year-old CEO of KPMG, a multinational accounting and business services firm, and was diagnosed with advanced cancer. They gave him ninety days to live, and he died exactly ninety days after the diagnosis. On their own, both books were awesome, but what was so remarkable is that when I jotted down the themes of both books, they were identical. Two completely different authors and situations, yet both basically arrived at the same conclusions about death and dying. Here are the ones that jumped out at me:

1. The end of your life can be the best part of your life.

2. Death can be experienced as a blessing, not a curse.

3. Death is not about hanging on, but about acceptance, surrender, and letting go.

4. Death leads you to focus on energy management rather than time management; energy is the life force within you.

5. In death, the only thing you have is now.

6. Death provides you with carefree timelessness or allows you to create perfect moments in the life without being conscious of time at all.

7. Death evokes simplicity—you are freed of all the stuff you've accumulated.

8. In dying we find a connection to nature and water.

9. Death underscores the value of love, divine love, and oneness.

10. We never, ever truly die.

I shared these thoughts with Sister Camille one day when we took a long walk on a trail overlooking Lake Michigan. We came to a bench and sat down, taking in the beauty of one of the largest bodies of fresh water on the planet. From previous discussions we'd had about death and dying, I felt free to share with her from these two books, neither of which were overtly religious, at least not in a traditional sense. With a gentle breeze cooling us from the August heat, I pulled a sheet of paper from my coat pocket and read her those ten observations. After I finished reading, she sat quietly for a few moments, looking across the water as if she was trying to see a boat in the distance. From previous experiences, I knew that she was pondering every word; running them through the filter of what she had been taught, what she believed.

"You know dearie, in a way, we're all dying. We just don't know when. So, what you just read applies to all of us, no matter how old we are, if we're in good health or have a terminal illness. They just described how all of us should approach life, not just when death seems close."

In her typical modern-day saint fashion, she took the wisdom of those two authors, processed it from her unique perspective, and turned it upside-down without changing a thing. She was basically telling me that death is not about dying but about living. That we should live every day as if it our last day on this planet. That's really the only way to live. She reminded me that in the only sermon recorded in the Bible that Jesus preached, he urged his followers not to be anxious about tomorrow, but to live each day content with whatever you have. Carefree timelessness?

As we revisited the concept of death, I played a recording of Wayne Dyer where he talks candidly about death. A lot of religious people question his teachings, but I think he's awesome. This time we were sitting in a little lounge in Clare Hall, and I secretly wondered if I might get struck by lightning for playing the recording in such a sacred space. But I played it anyway. Sister listened intently, may I say religiously, closing her eyes as Dyer concluded his meditation:

"I now turn away from the ego; withdraw into the depths of my being to the immortal consciousness that lies within. Here in this magic center, my word is law. I need only speak it with faith and conviction, and it will manifest in my life. I am calm and serene. Sure and unfaltering. For my roots are in eternity. All the things of life shall change and pass away. But I shall never pass away, for wherever life is I shall be. One with universal subconscious mind. I need not strive or strain to achieve immortality nor fear punishment, nor aspire for reward. The kingdom of heaven awaits all. The wise, the foolish. The sinner. And the saint. For we are all one in reality. Clothed in different forms in this moment of incarnation. I do not fear death. For by it I attain the consciousness of higher self. Neither do I invite death, for it must wait until my work is done. I forsake the ego, receive self in self. See the majesty, the grandeur, and the immortality of the power that dwells within. Amen." (from *Three Magic Words,* by Uell S. Andersen read by Wayne Dyer).

I turned off the recorder and asked her what she thought of this passage that didn't exactly conform to what I had been taught about heaven and hell. She thought for a moment, and then surprised me with her answer.

"I think what your friend Mr. Dyer says is quite close to what I believe," she began. "I completely agree with his observation that we never pass away, and I like the way he explains that our roots are in eternity."

She went on to acknowledge that her deceased sister Joanne has never left her. As she put it, Sister Joanne may have discarded her "worn out coat," that was her body, but her soul lives on.

"I talk to Joanne every day," she told me. I agree with Mr. Dyer that wherever life is I will be. As long as I'm connected to a light that shines through all of us, I'll never die." So, I said to her, "Sister, if you transition before me, would you (at the right time) throw down a rope and pull me up to you?"

She said, "I don't have to, dearie. We are already connected to our Creator and each other." Then she gave me that mischievous smile and winked at me.

I love Sister's image of discarding a worn-out coat. Our culture focuses so much attention on our physical bodies that when we die, we think that's the end. It's only the end for our bodies. The essence of who we are lives on forever. That's what enables Camille to talk with her sister, Joanne. It's what gives me the pleasure of consulting with members of my "virtual board of directors" who are deceased. I just can't believe that one of those board members, the late Mr. Rogers, was meant to be with us for only the seventy-five years that his body lived on this earth. When I'm wrestling with a leadership issue, I go to him for advice. Or if I need advice on humility, I consult the late John Wooden.

Although Sister appeared to appreciate and even agree with some of my unconventional (to some) thoughts about death and dying, she always reminded me that no one knows for sure what life after death will be like. Her faith, however, gave her the reassurance that whatever happens to us after we die, it will be perfect. In her words, our attitude as we approach our final days should be that of "a trustful surrender." Don't fight it. Don't fear it. When it is your appointed time to die, you will transition to an eternal existence of perfection.

Her attitude about death reminded me of something I read that was attributed to Chief Tecumseh, the great Shawnee warrior:

"When it comes time to die, be not like those whose hearts are filled with fear of death, so that when their time comes, they weep and pray for a little more time to live their lives over and over again in a different way. Sing your death song and die like a hero going home."

Sometimes I think animals understand death better than we do. I like watching some of the videos on cable television and recall one where an alligator had attacked a deer. The deer fought valiantly for a few minutes, then just gave up. In a few gulps, she was gone. Probably not the most appealing analogy, but think about it. All our lives we struggle to succeed, make more money, raise a family, get involved in our communities. Then we get a tough diagnosis and even though it looks hopeless, we fight like hell because we don't want to die. Of course, we don't, and I'd probably fight some myself. But at some point, we have to accept the inevitable, not as some horrible ending, but as the beginning of something new and exciting.

On a practical level, Sister's belief that we never die enabled her to cope with the deaths of her friends and loved ones. When her sister died, I don't recall seeing any tears. The funeral was truly a celebration of a life well lived, not a sorrowful event commemorating someone who was no longer with us. To Sister, Joanne was as alive as the rest of us, and knowing that allowed her to move forward without the debilitating grief many experience when someone passes. When I stopped by her house a couple of days after Joanne's funeral, Sister Camille was on going through her sister's clothes and meager possessions, deciding which ones to keep and which to donate to someone who might need them. Her demeanor was the same as it was before the funeral, and when I asked how she was doing, she replied with a smile, "It was her time. There are seasons for everything, and this was her season to transition into something better."

Life goes on.

I keep a can of A&W root beer in my office. When I was a kid, I loved A&W root beer, but I don't drink it anymore. Too much sugar. So why do I keep a can of it around? To remind me of one of the most profound truths I learned from Sister Camille about death and dying. At first it didn't make any sense.

"You know dearie, you can actually die before you die."

Huh? First, she reminds me that we never die. Now she's telling me we can die before we die. Is she just playing with me? Then in her typical way, she bowled me over with her wisdom.

"If you can detach yourself from all the things that hold you to this world (Can you let go of your possessions, identity, and your ego?), then you gain the capacity to look at your transition into the next with awe and wonder."

A&W.

This is how sister lived. With awe and wonder over what was ahead. She held loosely the artifacts of her life. Her degrees. Her accomplishments, which were many. Her struggles, as well as her joys. I once heard of a speaker who asked his audience to take a sheet of paper and make a dot on the upper left-hand corner. Then draw a line underneath the dot that stretched all across the page, and to imagine it continuing on toward infinity.

"The dot represents the seventy or eighty years most of us can expect to live. Most of us live for the dot. But the line represents the eternity that awaits."

He paused to let that sink in, then added.

"Don't live for the dot; live for the line."

Sister lived for the line. She knew that so much more awaited her; why cling to the tiny blip of time that we spend on this planet? She had learned how to die before she died so that she could look to the future with awe and wonder. It is how I try to live, and I would encourage you to try and do the same. Dying before you die is the only way to live.

When she shared that concept with me, I scrolled through my cellphone and found what I knew I had to share with her. It's the fiftieth verse of the *Tao Te Ching*. We had read it together many times, and she often remarked how much it meant to her. In her little apartment in Clare Hall, I set the phone on an end table, and we stood across from each other, both her hands held in mine:

Between birth and death,
three in ten are followers of life;
three in ten are followers of death.
And men just passing from birth to death
also number three in ten.
Why is this so?
Because they clutch to life
and cling to this passing world.
But there is one in ten, they say, so sure of life
that tigers and wild bulls keep clear.
Weapons turn from him on the battlefield,
rhinoceroses have no place to horn him,
tigers find no place for claws,
and soldiers have no place to thrust their blades.
Why is this so?
Because he dwells in that place
where death cannot enter.
Realize your essence
and you will witness the end without ending.

Sister Camille was the one in ten that dwelled in that place where death could not enter.

— 18 —

SAYING GOODBYE

After I left the motherhouse that Thursday night, when it was clear Sister Camille was nearing the end of her remarkable earthly journey, I drove home, wondering if I would ever see her again in this life. Physically, she had grown alarmingly weak, though her mind was as sharp and clear as ever. Normally, I shut my phone off before I go to bed, but I left it on just in case someone from the motherhouse should call. The nuns had grown increasingly protective of her, but I still had a few allies. I knew one of them would call if Sister took a turn for the worse.

When I awoke Friday morning, the first thing I did was check my phone in case maybe I had slept through an incoming call. Nothing, which was good news to me. Sister must still be holding on. I had some work to do at the office, but my heart wasn't in it. These were sacred moments, and I didn't want to miss out. I decided my work could wait, left the office, and drove to the motherhouse.

As I headed south on Lake drive and saw the waves building on Lake Michigan, I recalled the many times we watched those waves together, almost overwhelmed by their beauty and power. I recalled how I'd read how nature and water brought comfort to those who were dying and wished I could carry her to the water's edge and give her one more glimpse of one of her favorite scenes from nature. You would think that the drive to the motherhouse would be somber, flooding my soul with dread. I knew that I was about to lose my closest friend, but to be honest, I was actually singing that Billy Joel song "She's Got a Way," that I mentioned earlier.

For me, this wasn't a sad song, because I knew from my many conversations with Sister that I would never have to live without her. She would be just as present to me after she transitioned as she was at any of our lunches or dinners together. Still, I was eager to see her one more time before she passed, and I just had this feeling that this might be my last visit with her. It's sort of ironic in a way, because that was the emotion I felt every time I was on my way to see her: eagerness. This time was no different.

I turned onto the long, tree-lined driveway leading through the campus of the Archdiocese of Milwaukee past St. Francis de Sales Seminary and parked in front of Clare Hall. I half expected to see her standing at the entrance, waiting for me to pick her up and take her to one of her favorite neighborhood restaurants. I smiled to myself as I remembered the first time we had lunch together and she ordered her trademark martini. "Wow—this nun knows what she likes," I thought to myself at the time. She may have been a nun, pledging her entire life to serving God, but she was also very human. She loved life to the fullest, enjoying pleasures great or small. She could get just as excited watching the birds at her feeder as she did when she handed out diplomas to the graduating seniors under her care.

I walked the short distance to the motherhouse, and as I approached the entrance, I knew something was up. Instead of the lone attendant at the receptionist's desk, a group of about six or seven nuns had gathered, literally blocking the entrance to the hall that would take me to Sister's residence.

"I'm sorry, Mr. Sweeney, but Sister isn't seeing any visitors," one of the more officious nuns announced as I started to make my way down the hallway. I'm pretty sure I heard one of the other nuns whisper, "But he's her best friend." Didn't matter. It was made clear to me that I wasn't going to be able to see Sister Camille that day, which probably meant I would never see her again in this life.

"You're welcome to go to the chapel and pray for her soul," Sister Busybody offered.

"Thank you, Sister. I believe I'll do that."

Like hell I would. I headed down another hall that would take me to one of the two chapels in the motherhouse, but once I was out of their sight I slipped out a side door. In my many visits to the motherhouse, I'd gotten to know the lay of the land, so to speak. I walked around to the back of the building, found the entrance I was looking for, checked to see that no one saw me, then quickly ducked inside and found a back stairway seldom used and climbed up to the floor of my beloved friend's residence.

It worked. The two nuns and a nurse in Sister's room must have thought Sister Busybody made an exception for me and stood aside, so I could walk up close to Sister's bed.

"Hi Sister," I greeted. "It's me, Joe. You don't have to say anything. I just want you to know I'm here."

Her eyes were closed; she didn't respond. That was fine, but what wasn't was that her breathing was labored. Clearly, she was struggling, not to hang on, but just to breathe. I stepped over to the nurse and asked if she could give Sister something to make her more comfortable. I knew from previous experiences with people in their final stages that it was quite common to administer sedatives to make the patient as comfortable as possible. Before the nurse could respond, one of the nuns jumped in.

"Oh, we can't do that, Mr. Sweeney."

"Why not?" I asked.

"That would only speed things up; we need to do everything we can to spare her life."

I couldn't believe what I was hearing. I knew and even respected the Catholic view of life being sacred and that we should do all we can to preserve and protect it. But Sister Camille was ninety-five. Unconscious. She'd lived a good life of total commitment to her faith. And she was ready to go. I just wanted her to be more comfortable, not speed anything up. But I honored the nun's wishes and stood by Sister's bed.

Apparently, I was deemed safe enough to be left alone with Sister Camille, as the nurse and nuns stepped out of the apartment. I pulled a chair up next to the bed and, over the next thirty minutes or so, spoke gently to her.

"It's okay to go."

"I'll bet Joanne's so excited to see you again."

"I love you Sister Camille."

"We had some great times, didn't we?"

"It's okay to go."

I felt helpless watching her struggle so. It was then that I thought to pray the prayer we had said so many times together.

"The light of God shines through us. The love of God flows through us. We are rooted in Divine love for eternity. And so, it is." She never responded, and my hunch is that even though she was still breathing, she was on her way. I reached for her hand with both of mine and kissed it.

"Goodbye Sister."

And then I left.

It takes about twenty minutes to get from the motherhouse to my home, and all I could think as I drove was what a lucky guy I was to have known Sister Camille. The great American philosopher and psychologist William James once observed that "The great use of life is to spend it on something that will outlast it." Sister generously poured her life into not only mine, but literally thousands of other students, faculty, civic leaders, rich, poor, and forgotten. I'm one of many who can say with complete honesty, I am a better person because of her.

It was late when I pulled into my driveway. I looked over my mail, answered a few voicemails, the climbed into bed. Once again, I left my phone on in case anything happened in the night.

It did.

Around 4:30 in the morning, my phone rang. It was Sister K.D. I could tell by the quiver in her voice and the time of night that Sister had transitioned to the next life.

"Joe, I thought you should know. Sister passed just a few minutes to go. You're the first that I've called."

"Thank you, Sister," I responded. "Please tell all the sisters that they are in my prayers."

Nine days after she transitioned, I joined a packed chapel in Clare Hall to celebrate Sister's remarkable life. It was a lovely tribute, with beautiful music, prayers, eulogies, and her beloved number 21 Kliebhan Packer jersey. I spoke briefly, sharing how Sister had made such an impact on me. When the service was over, I got in line to pay my respects to Sister. As I bent to kiss her, I knew that this was only the "discarded coat" that she left behind. She was already catching up with Joanne, hanging out with her mom and dad once again.

Her favorite Packer jersey, number 21. It was her uncle's number as one of the first Green Bay Packer quarterbacks. He lost his job to the famous Curly Lambeau.

Richard Rohr once wrote, "Wherever there is union, there is a little bit of heaven." For thirty years, I was privileged to enjoy a unique and special union with Sister Camille. I know we talk about heaven as being "up there" somewhere, but whenever I had the opportunity to be with Sister, I experienced that little bit of heaven that Fr. Rohr described.

A few months later on a brutally cold February afternoon, I drove to the little cemetery where Sister had been buried. I came in the back way, a route I'd never taken before, parked my car, and walked over to her gravesite. I laid down in the snow beside her grave and talked with her for a while, then got up to leave when something caught my eye. From where I was standing, I looked directly at the cross on her headstone. But I saw another cross. One etched by the late afternoon sun setting in the west. At that precise moment, the rays of light cast a giant shadow over Sister Camille's grave. In the shape of a cross. The sacred symbol of the faith she had carried throughout her life on earth. It was almost as if she was sending me a message. Then it dawned on me; the rope I asked her to throw down to me to stay connected was completely unnecessary. The light she so emanated in life continued to guide me in signs everywhere including her final resting place.

The cross reflected by the noon day sun on a garage above Sister Camille's grave

I repeated our prayer one last time.

"The light of God shines through us. The love of God flows through us. We are rooted in Divine Love for eternity." I could hear her soothing, steadfast voice reciting it with me. When we finished, I remembered what she once said to me.

"Death ends life for our bodies, but not our relationships."

The frigid wind that constantly blew the whole time I was standing by her grave curiously stopped briefly, and in the calm and silenced, I felt her words flow into my soul.

"I'm just fine, dearie. Take care. We will meet again soon . . . very soon."

EPILOGUE

A dear friend, Scott Stoner, shared a story with me recently, and it is so beautiful that I'd like to share it with you:

A historic cathedral was widely known for two things—it's magnificent stained glass windows depicting Biblical stories along with many of the saints and its commitment to offering an exceptional children's sermon every Sunday of the year.

One beautiful, sunny All Saints' Day the pastor asked all the children to come forward as he began to tell them some stories about what All Saints' Day celebrates. At one point, he paused and asked the kids, "Can anyone tell me what a saint is?" The kids were stumped—after all it's not an easy thing to define exactly what a saint is. Finally, after a long a pause, a young child looked up and saw the sun streaming through the stained-glass windows and proclaimed, "A saint is one of those people that the light shines through!"

No truer description or definition has ever been offered. Saints are those people who the Light shines through.

There may not yet be a stained-glass window of Sister Camille, but clearly, she is a person that the Light shone through. My hope in sharing this book with you and sharing the Light that shone through Sister Camille is that this same Light may now shine just a little brighter through you."

Celebrating Sister's 93rd birthday.
Peace be with you dear Sister Camille, a modern-day saint if there ever was one.

APPENDIX

— Daily or Morning Prayers —

TOP FOURTEEN STATIONS

Begin by using 4-2-4 Breathing, or inhaling for four seconds, hold for two seconds, and release for four seconds

1. G.O.W. I AM grateful, open, and willing. Lead me today where you need me most!

   Open the door and I will walk through it. (Ben Carson)

   I AM open to everything and attached to nothing.

   "I live no longer, not I; but Christ lives in me" (Galatians 2:20)

   Whatever days are left in me, belong to him. Ronald Reagan

2. Holy Spirit BE HERE NOW. Come, Holy Spirit, I invite you into the very depths of my being. Lead me, guide me, coach me, encourage me and challenge me. Direct me in all things. Teach me to become a great decision maker, so that in every moment of every day I can choose what is good, right, noble and just.

3. I AM strong, healthy, prosperous and free through the actions of God working through me.

   Stay connected to the vine.

   Read: I the Vine you are the branches. Stay connected to me.

4. Make me a channel for your love and peace. Recite the prayer of St. Francis.

   Lord, make me an instrument of Thy peace;Where there is hatred, let me sow love;Where there is injury, pardon;Where there is doubt, the faith;Where there is despair, hope;Where there is darkness, light;And where there is sadness, joy.O Divine Master, Grant that I may not so much seek to be consoled, as to console;To be understood, as to understand;To be loved as to love.For it is in giving that we receive;It is in pardoning that we are pardoned;And it is in dying that we are born to eternal life.Amen.

5. I surround you with light and love. As I do myself.

   Do this with Loved ones, kids, daughters in law and grand kids. Walk through day and bless everyone I plan to encounter and others that I may meet.

   Choose 10 people every morning and do this exercise for them.

6. Water of life AM I poured forth for thirsty men. Drink 100 ounces of water a day.

   Earth 75% water bodies 75% water brains 85% water.

7. I AM living and flowing in the abundance of God.

   $, people and resources

   The light of God shines through me. The love of God flows through me. I am rooted in the house of the Lord for eternity.

8. God - help me to help others become the best version of themselves. My fruit grows on other people's trees.

   Lord, create a Safeway to bring Joe into a world class team and to help him find/belong to something bigger than himself.

9. I live in the GAP. Gratitude = Abundance + Prosperity.

   I establish myself in the amazing abundance of the One Universal Mind.

   I am so grateful for the Abundance and Prosperity that I blessed with at every minute at every hour of every day.

10. My 3 core I AMs. Do the ABC....

    I Am Grateful leads to abundance.

    I AM Humble leads to service.

    I AM Inspiring. Leads to helping others to be the best version of themselves. G.H.I.

11. I came from GREATNESS. Tao, God. I AM what I came from. I will never abandon the belief in my own greatness and the greatness of others.

12. Practice detachment of my possessions, people, my body.

13. Convene and communicate with the virtual board.

    All 6 groups.

14. Release. Let Go and let God. Stay connected to the Universe and the Divine Mind. Our Sacred Contract is to stay connected to the Divine.

8 QUESTIONS TO ASK YOURSELF EVERY DAY

1. What's the best thing I experienced today?

2. How did I do today to live my ideal day?

3. What was one new thing that I learned today?

4. How did God work through me today?

5. What am I most grateful for today?

6. What did I do to inspire others?

7. What am I most looking forward to tomorrow?

8. What did I do today to create a belly laugh?

PRAYER OF ST. FRANCIS

Lord, make me an instrument of Thy peace;

Where there is hatred, let me sow love;

Where there is injury, pardon;

Where there is doubt, the faith;

Where there is despair, hope;

Where there is darkness, light;

And where there is sadness, joy.

O Divine Master, grant that I may not so much seek to be consoled as to console; to be understood as to understand; to be loved as to love.

For it is in giving that we receive; it is in pardoning that we are pardoned, and it is in dying that we are born to eternal life.

Amen.

ABOUT THE AUTHOR

Joe Sweeney has spent more than 35 years blending his love of business with his passion for sports. He has owned, operated, and sold several manufacturing companies, headed up the Wisconsin Sports Authority, and launched a sports marketing firm representing professional athletes and coaches. He also owned equity interest and managed an investment banking firm and is currently a private equity investor serving on numerous boards of directors.

Sweeney is an accomplished *New York Times* best-selling author, internationally known speaker, and investor in private equity companies. Along the way, he has sought meaning and purpose from his own faith as well as from the teachings of spiritual leaders.

To contact Joe Sweeney, visit his website at https://www.joesweeney.com.

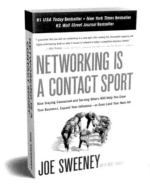
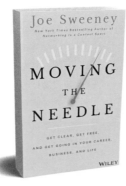